MAKE IT HAPPEN

A GUIDE TO MAKING YOUR DREAMS COME TRUE

MIGUEL SANCHEZ

Miguel Sanchez

Make It Happen

Make

It

Happen

By: Miguel Sanchez

Miguel Sanchez

Make It Happen

Copyright © 2021 by Trient Press

All rights reserved. No part of this publication may be reproduced, distributed, or transmitted in any form or by any means, including photocopying, recording, or other electronic or mechanical methods, without the prior written permission of the publisher, except in the case of brief quotations embodied in critical reviews and certain other noncommercial uses permitted by copyright law. For permission requests, write to the publisher, addressed "Attention: Permissions Coordinator," at the address below.

Criminal copyright infringement, including infringement without monetary gain, is investigated by the FBI and is punishable by up to five years in federal prison and a fine of $250,000.

Except for the original story material written by the author, all songs, song titles, and lyrics mentioned in the novel The Silent Wars are the exclusive property of the respective artists, songwriters, and copyright holder.

Trient Press
3375 S Rainbow Blvd
#81710, SMB 13135
Las Vegas,NV 89180

Ordering Information:
Quantity sales. Special discounts are available on quantity purchases by corporations, associations, and others. For details, contact the publisher at the address above.
Orders by U.S. trade bookstores and wholesalers. Please contact Trient Press: Tel: (775) 996-3844; or visit www.trientpress.com.

Printed in the United States of America

Publisher's Cataloging-in-Publication data
Sanchez, Miguel
A title of a book :make It Happen

ISBN Hardcover : 978-1-953975-75-1
    Paperback : 978-1-955198-03-5
    E-book   : 978-1-955198-04-2

Miguel Sanchez

Make It Happen

Dedication

I want to dedicate this book to first and foremost my mother (**Sylvia McNeil**), Eric Price, Sylvia Quinton, my cousin Charles Douglas, my frat brothers' Kimmer Young, John Ervin, and Shawn Jenkins. When the chips are truly down, that's when you find out who your true friends are. Special thanks to my cousin Sharon Taylor who always told me I was a millionaire

Miguel Sanchez

Introduction

For those of you who may be stuck in dead end jobs or feel as though their lives are not moving forward. This book is for you. It took me years to figure out what true happiness consists of and how to achieve it. This book is designed for you to "Make it happen" in whatever area of your life you'd like.

To me –being devoid of money is like walking around with sand in your underwear! It's irritating and I can't stand it! So I wrote this book to try to help those people who wanted to make a change in their life actually happen, not just to make money- but for relationships, spiritual life, health changes, just about anything you want to change …you can "Make it Happen"!

For most of my adult life I have wondered why some people fail and others succeed. I have studied it, sought it, researched it, prayed on it and pondered on the reasons. This book is an assimilation of my thoughts

Miguel Sanchez

on why I believe so many of us seem to fall short of finding our true purpose for our own individual existence.

I believe that - we as individuals-are all special. We are all advocates for ourselves, and if we are so special why are most of us not pursuing that thing that makes us so special. So why are we here? What could possibly be the purpose for your existence? Each one of us has a destiny to fulfill, and this journey that we're on has -in my opinion- 2 factions to it. To find our purpose and execute it, and ultimately to help others find theirs and to help them execute their purposes.

Whether this book sells 1 copy (well I know it will sell 1 because my Mother will buy that 1) or a million. Hopefully it will inspire and help you to become what you are meant to be. I want to share with you some of my experiences in life and what I believe are hindrances that keep us from truly obtaining the results we seek in ourselves. I am speaking of that person that we want to or wish to become. What is the driving force that holds us from us? Fear has a great deal to do with it but there are some basic habits that we unconsciously take on that hold us from ultimately having the

Make It Happen

abundance that God wants us to have. **And I mean all of us to have.**

The majority of us have some sort of routine that we go through on a daily basis and have been for some time. The routine can begin to form as early as your teens but (in my opinion) for most people it begins in your 30's or 40's. We create families; careers and have bills and so on. We seem to settle into a life and lifestyle that simply "pays the bills". You see, I don't believe that any child says to themselves, "when I grow up, I want to work for the state". I am simply using it as an example of unconscious behavior which I will get more into throughout the book.

What I am trying to say is that somehow we sometimes- as human beings- we gravitate to find an occupation that we didn't necessarily ever think we would be in, but because of the situation we were in at the time, led us to that job or lifestyle and we just kind of "settle into it because it " paid the bills" or it's what I need to do for right now until I can do better.

Miguel Sanchez

Unfortunately for quite a few of us better never materializes. We say " I'll wait until the children are in school – then its I'll wait until the kids graduate – then it's the grand kids that hold us up and so on and so on.

What I hope to accomplish in writing this- is that I am able to say something or impart some parcel of knowledge through my own hiccups throughout life, combined with the study of success (that I have been doing for almost 25 years now) and hope that you're able to get something from it.

Some people sell cars, others sell all kinds of goods and services. People who write (some) books are merely selling you on their own thoughts or some research that they've done or some experience that they've had. They are simply taking the time out of their busy days and putting those results on paper for you to judge for yourself whether it be their thoughts, research or experiences, they are selling you something you are willing to pay for. And you ask, isn't that what you're doing? Well yes if you must know! However I don't want

Make It Happen

to just motivate you – I want you to actually take action! You see part of the purpose of this book is to help you find a way to achieve the type of success that you thought may have been unobtainable but to also to become fully aware of your circumstances and alter them if you so choose to. Part of my own path to what I believe I needed to accomplish is to do something that I've wanted to do for years, and that is to put my thoughts and research on paper. This book is very simply about how to go about the business of becoming that person that you are supposed to be. The writing of this book is simply a part of my own process in becoming who I am supposed to be. I hope that these thoughts. ideas and facts do the same for you.

I initially dedicated this book to 3 people. They were not the sources of my information but merely the source of the catalyst that inspired me to regurgitate what existed within me ...always. In other words these individuals helped me realize that it was time to get up off of my posterior and take action. You will run into these people (if you haven't already), or you will find

Miguel Sanchez

that person, place or thing that brings out that which was always there in you- sooner or later. This book is meant for you to find that entity faster, or if you haven't found that thing that motivates you, then this book will help to teach you how to manufacture it so that causes *you to take action to become that person who you have always wanted to be... but just don't know it* yet.

Make It Happen

Table of Contents

Chapter One	What drives you?
Chapter Two	Finding your Purpose
Chapter Three	Turn off the T.V.!
Chapter Four	What does it take to achieve success
Chapter Five	How do you get motivated- and Stay that way!
Chapter Six	Breaking the cycle of Mediocrity
Chapter Seven	The spiritual side of success
Chapter Eight	The pursuit of happiness
Chapter Nine	Time Management

Miguel Sanchez

Make It Happen

Chapter One

What drives you?

Charles Kingsley said "We act as though comfort and luxury were the chief requirements of life when all we need to make us happy is something to be enthusiastic about".

One of the people I admire so dearly in life is Oprah Winfrey (among many others). As I am writing this book Oprah is on the cover of Fortune Magazine with an article on her new network she is about to launch. Many of us know the story about how she was molested as a child, or we got a chance to watch the interview tape of her to be on the show that she is now so well known for. But was is it that truly drives her or inspires her? It's obviously not money; she has more of that than she can possibly spend in one lifetime. Yet every day she gets up and goes to work when she obviously doesn't have to work at all? Why do it? And why do it in Chicago (where it's freezing)? If I were as

Miguel Sanchez

wealthy as her I would want to wake up in a place where it was warm and sunny every day. We all know how cold it can get in Chicago! My thoughts are simply this. **Oprah doesn't go to work...she goes to play**. When you have truly found why God has placed you on this planet, you never have to work another day in your life! When you get up in the morning and go do what you were born to do, what you love to do ...what you would do for free...then you have truly found your passion. When your passion for that thing burns so deeply inside of you that it causes you anxiety and because you crave it so bad and, because you crave it and you want it and you are able to do that thing you do so well, then what begins to happen is - the money just seems to flow in ...just like Oprah.

So how do we find that thing that Oprah has found, or Steve Jobs, Warren Buffet, Barak Obama, Nelson Mandela, Bill and Hillary Clinton, Bill Cosby, Michael Jackson and on and on. What truly makes the great, great (By the way, I read that book too by Dennis Kimbro)? But better yet how can you or I tap into whatever it is that **they** have tapped into or even a small portion in order to experience some semblance of what **they** have found. You can't choose your purpose- your purpose is something that is **discovered-not learned**. Since you were little you have been drawn to certain activities and ways that you do things and as time goes by it will become clearer and clearer to you what is unique- to just you. It reveals itself in a very subtle tone(at first), but if you (Hone in on) that voice then it becomes easier and easier to hear it.

This is what I have pondered on, and studied for oh so many years as to what I needed or was lacking in order to "be like Mike". The answer is simple -but it took 25 years to figure it out. You or I don't need to" be like Mike" – we need to be like ourselves. None of those people are the same or similar to anyone else. They are themselves. They aren't trying to be like anything or anyone else but who they already are. They have tapped into exactly who and what GOD has meant for them to be and then exploited it. They know exactly why they are here. If you don't believe me just ask them, except for MJ and Steve Jobs (god rest their souls). So how do we do that? Not only how do we do that, but how do we do it consistently and create whatever we want for ourselves instantly? If you don't really know what drives you then how do you find out? How do we find our purpose? There are many books on how we do it, but if so many people have written books on it and told us how to do it, then why is it that we all haven't reached that self-actualization point? Why we not all wealthy are, spiritually fulfilled, healthy, and living in the Paradise that God intended like Adam and Eve.

The reasons are quite simple-we become and do what we put focus on. If you spend time meditating and focusing on increasing our awareness of ourselves then who we are and what we should become, and are here to do, becomes a great deal easier when we understand ourselves.

I was driving through Los Angeles and noticed as I was driving that a great deal of the houses in the city were very close to each other. By close I don't mean proximity, what I mean is that most of us are living very similar lifestyles. Yes there are always exceptions on either side of the coin-Some extremely wealthy and

Make It Happen

some extremely poor. But for the most part we are all living very close to the same way that the person next door to us lives. Why is that? Why can't we all have our own Airplane, or Yachts, or huge houses, healthy strong bodies, and be spiritually fulfilled? Why can't we all have wonderful relationships? Why do we consistently never seem to be able to break through to higher levels that we've never been to before? The fact is...is that you can! Not only can you ,but you can have more , do more, and become more of what ever thought you could ever think you'd be capable of. You just need the information and system to show you how.

If there is any one thing that I would like for this book to accomplish it would be to give people a blueprint or a template to success. There used to be a time when, even if you didn't have a college education or just a high school diploma, you could go to work in a plant or a factory and could still grind out a decent life and even buy a house. But those jobs have been shipped overseas and America is faced with a new era of families struggling to survive and/or make it to the next level. I hope that I am able to , in some way shape or form, help someone to adapt the principles, techniques, and habits of successful individuals in order that you may duplicate the same results in your own life. Sometimes it takes major catastrophic events to occur in your life to find the motivation to go out and accomplish that thing you were meant to accomplish. We don't necessarily want for you to have to go there for you achieve your dreams. Martin Luther King Jr. was motivated by a young woman by the name of Rosa Parks that helped him to start the "Montgomery Improvement Association" after a one day bus boycott was successful. That one event was enough to start the ball rolling on the civil rights movement that changed this country forever. What is it in you that could change your life forever?

In order to find what drives you, you have to spend some type of time focusing on that issue alone. Take the time to write down some of the things in your life that you enjoy doing or that you find yourself doing without even thinking about it. What excites you? When you're in the car alone where does your mind drift to? If your mind drifts to your daily problems and what you have going on right now then use that time between

Make It Happen

destinations to analyze what motivates you. Train your mind to use time wisely to help you to elevate yourself from one level to the next. This is step one on the journey to success. This first step will save you countless hours, days , months or even years of wasted time and effort spending it aimlessly searching for what you were placed here on earth to do. Become conscious of what you think about . Think about what you think about. This book is actually an interruption in what your thoughts are – use the information given here to interrupt your thoughts on a daily basis as a way of disrupting the deep rooted habits that you've formed up to this point in your life.

Miguel Sanchez

Chapter Two

Finding your Purpose

One of the greatest tragedies in this day and time in the history of this nation (to me) is that so few people are engaged in the work for which they are best suited. We live in a time like no other time in the history of mankind where information is instantaneously available, literally at the touch of a button. At any moment we can talk to another person who is halfway around the world from us. We can "Google" the world's information in a millisecond. Think if Einstein, Thomas Edison, Sir Isaac Newton, or any one of a host of great thinkers and inventors had the access to the information that we have now, what they could or would have done with it?

Yet we lack the ability or capability to figure out what the one thing is on this earth that our existence was meant to pursue? In order for true lasting success to take place, you must find what your true purpose is. You must do this first among all things in order not to waste your time, energy and efforts in pursuing goals

Miguel Sanchez

that are not congruent with your specific ability to do what you do best. Each and every time that I pray over my food, I pray that I will use the energy that the food provides for me to pursue my ultimate destiny without wasting the energy it provides.

There is some one thing that you can do that no one else in this world can do better than you. Focus all of your energy and effort into finding out what that thing is and then use that thing to obtain your purpose and ultimate goal and be not distracted in the pursuit of it.

To me the richest piece of Real Estate on earth is the cemetery, because so many of us die with so much left in us to give.

Someone once said that "The 2 most important days in your life are...the day you were born and the day you find out why you were born".

So many of us never follow through with that idea, write that book, open that business, or create that invention. So how do we go about fulfilling our purpose? The very first step in becoming who we were meant to be is figuring out what gifts we have come to be blessed with. Not only what gifts we are blessed with but also how to become that person. Also what do I need to do today, or tomorrow morning to find out who I am actually suppose to be and why I showed up here at this very moment in time.

To begin, a psychologist (Gordon Allport) believed that there are over 4,000 different personality characteristic traits that exist in human beings. There are over 7 Billion people on this planet and not one human being has the exact same mixture of character and personality traits of another human being. What this means is that each and every single one of us is a unique individual with different doses of skills, abilities, physical attributes, and so on. Infinite intelligence is not redundant; you are absolutely here for a reason. Your unique skills and abilities are …just that …unique. You alone have something to offer the world that no other human being can possibly offer…only you posses the combination of talents skills and abilities to bring about that thing in which you were brought here to do. So the question remains, "how do we find it, how do we begin to seek out this incredible gift that lies within". Someone

Miguel Sanchez once said that experience + reflection = wisdom. In order to gain wisdom (to assist you in finding your purpose) you must first begin by reflecting back on where you are right now in your life. You are where you are in your life at this very moment because of the decisions that you have made …or failed to make. It has also been said" that at some time you made an appointment to be exactly where you are today". You are where you are because of you…and no one else. You can blame the economy, the President, your environment, your upbringing or even your ex-wife or husband, but the real truth is, is that you will never be able to control what others do , you can only control what you do…or don't do. You can change the quality of your life almost immediately because God gave us 1 gift that all of us have in common, and that is that we all have the power of choice. Eleanor Roosevelt said that "Life is like a parachute jump, you only get one shot at it". There's no second chance. In order to begin to find our purpose we must use this power of choice to examine the choices we have made throughout our life and be very honest with ourselves and reflect on what got us here. When you rise tomorrow morning use that time to reflect back on the events, decisions, and circumstances that caused you to be in the circumstances that you find yourself currently in.

Now finding your purpose is the most important part of this entire book. Without finding that thing in which you were brought here to do you will go on feeling incomplete or not totally fulfilled. This is how we were created. So what we need is a method of going about finding our assignment here on earth. Here are a few tips on how to find that thing in which you were meant to find in yourself.

1) Ask yourself "What would you do if you knew that you could not fail"?
2) Ask yourself "What would you do for free"?
3) Whatever the thing is that you are supposed to do-you will be good at doing
4) Whatever that thing is that you were meant to do -you **will** be given the opportunity to do it
5) Whatever that thing is that you were meant to do – you **will** love to do it.

Miguel Sanchez

6) You can find clues to what you are good at by asking friends and family what seems to come easy to you that is hard for others.

Here is an example of something that you can do to help you to narrow down finding your purpose.

1) Imagine that you have all the money that you need: Millions and Millions of dollars. What would you do every day with your time if money was no object? This is something you need to spend time pondering. Imagine waking up tomorrow morning and you lived in your dream house, drove your dream car(s), your family was taken care of; you've traveled the world extensively and have everything you could ever want or need. What would you spend your time doing? What would your days be filled with? You might say nothing at all, and that you would relax, but believe me that would get old fast! Whatever you see yourself doing in that context will help lead you to finding the purpose you were put on this earth to do. Now you can make a plan to fulfill your purpose. Don't get a plan confused with fulfilling your purpose. Just as you have a

unique gift, so does this entire country. Answer me this, what is the purpose of America? What was it born to do? What does this country find easier to do than other countries are able to do. What can this country do on a consistent basis to ensure that it is moving towards its' ultimate destination? Answering those questions may be of assistance to every elected official that aspires to move this country towards its destiny. Otherwise we can spend our energy, resources and money, wasting time pursuing goals that are not actually intended for us to pursue but are merely plans that have nothing to do with this country's purpose here on earth . Plans by themselves do not necessarily lead you to your destiny, but plans tied in to your purpose... well that is an entirely different matter altogether and one of the most powerful tools on earth!

When I was seventeen years old I had an eleven year plan. At the end of that plan I was going to become a lawyer. I could tell you years in advance what I was going to be doing at almost any time on any date , up to

Miguel Sanchez

eleven years in the future. My plan was to attend Tuskegee Institute (the name at the time I attended) for 4 years. While I was there I intended on being in the R.O.T.C. program and become an officer and a pilot when I graduated. That way I could immediately go to work without the worry of having to look for a job because I was a Political Science Major. I would then spend 4 years in the military as a pilot and after I got out I would go to Law School for 3 years. Sounds like a great plan! Well at seventeen years old (my freshman year at Tuskegee) I was told that I now had a baby boy. For the next eleven years I struggled to complete my Bachelor's degree while working to support a child. I went in The Army (the 82nd Airborne , Ft. Bragg North Carolina) and completed my Bachelor's degree in order to take care of my son and finish college. As a matter of fact when my son turned 9 I took full custody of him and raised him from then on out(even today I'm still raising him , although he's well into his 40's now) It took me eleven years just to finish the first 4 years of the plan! The point is, is **that was a plan-not a purpose**. Don't get me wrong, there's nothing wrong with a plan but it's not a purpose. However a plan can help to get

Make It Happen

you to fulfilling your purpose if you know what that purpose is. Later on (when I reflected back) I found out that I knew that I would make my mother and my family very proud becoming a Lawyer. But when I really gave it some thought, would I enjoy the day to day work of what a lawyer actually does? Would I jump out of bed in the morning actually looking forward to what I had to do that day? My plan was to become a Lawyer, but that was not my calling and so my plan changed.

There's nothing wrong with failure. I will say this repeatedly throughout this book. Failure is merely a bi-product of success. It is necessary in order for you to achieve success. So don't be afraid of it, as a matter of fact you <u>want to welcome</u> failure and look at it as one step closer to your becoming successful. Without those failures you would not have known how not to do something. I heard a story once that a young man had inherited over $100 million dollars as a baby. He had servants to take care of him and bodyguards to make sure that no harm came to him. He didn't even have to dress himself because there were servants to do that for him. One day he was playing in the back yard of a house.

Miguel Sanchez

Somehow the gate was left open, and being that he was 10 years old, he had never ventured out past the gate without someone being there to watch him. This particular day, the servants and bodyguards were occupied with something else and as a curious young boy he decided to venture outside of the gate by himself. The moment that he did he was immediately hit by a car and was killed. He had never crossed the street on his own because he always had another set of eyes doing that for him. He was not allowed to go through the progression of struggle and strife that was typical of a human being in order for them to reach their own potential. We have to fail in order to succeed...

My Mother recently took a vacation to Bermuda (which is an oxymoron to me because she's already retired). On her way back she flew into Washington, D.C. (where we both grew up), and she ran into an old girlfriend of hers. The woman was married and was going on and on about how upset she was with her boyfriend, that's right I said boyfriend. So much so that she had keyed her boyfriend's car! The woman was 75 years old! This very same woman was the one that broke up the marriage of my mother and father over 50 years ago. She had not changed! The reason I tell this particular story is that this is truly an example of someone who had not taken the time to reflect on past experiences and was doomed on repeating the same thing over and over again. She was guilty of violating the first principle of finding your purpose in life. Tony Robbins said that the most powerful force for we humans, is the need or a desire to stay consistent with how we define ourselves. The question is- when did we establish this pattern, when we were teenagers, in our 20's, 30's …when? When I was a baby my name was still Miguel but as I grew older my prospective changed and it continues to change, and will continue to change as I continue to grow. When I am 97 I will still be trying to climb another mountain. That is how we are wired; we will never become happy by the obtaining of things. Russell Simmons said "that there is nothing under a hood of a car that will ever make us truly happy". **It is only in the becoming of who we are truly meant to be, that will ever make us content and fulfilled.**

So why does finding our purpose tend to allude most of us. Well one reason is, is that we haven't

Miguel Sanchez

spent the time reflecting as I mentioned earlier. Another reason is that in order to find that gift inside of yourself – you must find that thing that you do well. The thing in which you do well or that comes easier to you than to others is a place to start. When you listen to others that have spoken to you and have said that you seem to have a talent for that or how is it that something you're able to do comes so easy to you, but hard for others, is a great place to start. Again- this is a cornerstone to begin searching for that hidden element inside that drives you. You see by finding that thing inside you that have a talent for, gives you clue as to what your purpose is. The gift that you were given is tied directly to the purpose in to which you were intended to use it for. If you can draw or paint, then you have a creative gift that is somehow to be used in order to deliver the rest of us some sort of beauty or message which only you are going to be able to draw or paint. Only you have the unique experiences that you've been through, combined with your ability to paint or draw which enable only you to send a particular message(s) that you are able to send. You were not given a gift not to use it.

Make It Happen

Superman wasn't given his incredible powers in order not to be Superman!

There is nothing so wonderful to see than a person who is inspired and driven. There are examples of those types throughout history. Imagine the signers of the declaration of independence knowing that by signing that document, that if they were to lose, they would have sealed there death warrants. The evidence of their betrayal was right there on that document. That takes courage! That is why finding your purpose is absolutely the most important first step in becoming who you are supposed to become. Without knowing exactly what your purpose is you will lack the ultimate drive and passion you will inevitably need to break through to your self-actualization.

So what can you do today to find your purpose? As of right now you're already doing it. By reading this book, as well as others, you will begin to find the information that you need to ask yourself the right questions to find your true self. **You must start...by seeking understanding**. We become more intelligent through the books we read and the people we meet.

Miguel Sanchez

You can literally go to Barnes and noble tomorrow or any local book store and read up on personal development. You can Google the information that you need to help you supplement the information given to you here. This is exactly how I began to find my own purpose. I had to read. I read and read and read. And then I read some more. After a while it became apparent to me that success is very predictable and is simply a skill that needs to be acquired just like anything else. But first we must find out what our focus is going to be on.

Don't forget, if you knew everything there was to know, you'd be where you want to be. If you're not there yet then there is much more to learn. So read first in order to find your purpose. If you have to get up early before you go to work to be able to read then do it. Carve time out on Saturdays or on Sundays...but do it. If it is important to you, you will find a way to do it. If not you will find an excuse not to. Either way the choice is yours. Your future depends on it.

When I worked for a living I had a woman in my office that wanted to go to school to obtain her Associate Degree and already had a Bachelor's Degree.

Make It Happen

She told me that she was searching for her purpose. She was in her mid forties and had gotten a degree in Psychology. I informed her that a degree in any of the "ologies" was a hard skill to try and market unless you had an additional advanced Degree in today's competitive economy. She told me that she felt frustrated because she hadn't found what her reason for being here was yet. What I told her was this …She was frustrated because she felt as though she should have been on her way to towards her dreams. The real reason she was frustrated was because her opinion of where she thought she should be and where she actually was, conflicted with each other. For some people this is a source of deep depression. The problem with this thinking is that you can't be on your way if you don't know where you are going. Again every one of us all have gifts and talents that are unique to us. You cannot compare your unique abilities to that of another individual. Nor can you compare the time in which you allow yourself to achieve that dream to that of another human being with a different set of unique abilities. "A flower doesn't compare itself to another flower, it just blossoms".

Miguel Sanchez

If the infinite intelligence that created everything that we could ever see or know -the source that created me and you and and gave us dominion over all of it- why would that source not want us to have whatever it is that we wanted or desired. Why would it say "you can have dominion over this earth, but you can't have a Bentley , or Mercedes...or a new Bugatti ! What sense does that make?

I told her in order to find your purpose you must first write down everything that you could think of that you ever wanted in life and to leave no stone unturned. You must write down all of the possessions that you desire, the material objects, the places you wish to travel to, your relationships with your family, a greater connection with the higher source, and the type of relationship, everything without limitation. Once you have created this list then prioritize those things that you want or must do the most. Then list them in order of importance 1, 2,3,4,5 etc...Once you have your top ten then work on your next top ten. Of the top 10 then pick out the top 3 and you will be on your way to finding out what you really want and how to obtain what your true purpose is. This will help to give you the desire that

Make It Happen

you need to overcome any obstacle that you might come up against in the pursuit of your purpose.

    I believe that there are millions of Americans out there who are in these same or similar if the following situations. They are in their forties and working in a job that isn't what they want to do but is what they have to do in order to pay the bills. They are that person that has been working for the local state or government agency that has been there for years but still is not reaching their full potential. They are stuck in a world of going to work coming home cooking dinner, watching TV, and getting up in the morning and doing it all over again. They sleep walk through life, they are really dead already but just waiting for the day that they are to be buried. They don't know that all of us are extraordinary and that there is no one who is average... they've given up on the idea that they can still Make It Happen! . I want so desperately to get this point across to any of you who read this. that it doesn't have to be the way. You can change it and you can start doing it today! I once heard Denzel Washington say , while speaking to a group of aspiring actors that "True desire in the heart

Miguel Sanchez

for anything good is God's proof to you , sent beforehand ,to indicate... that it is yours already. He's indicating that if you had the propensity to think it – then you've already achieved it! Its there waiting for you, you already have what it takes to achieve your purpose. And also remember that Dreams without goals are just dreams... you have to put action behind them...

I caution you also to seek not a purpose that is strictly a way of obtaining material gain but rather to seek wisdom and understanding (sound familiar). I spent a great deal of my life learning about Real Estate investments, options trading, and opening up several different businesses in the search for wealth. Now I seek transitivity between myself and all that is knowable. The search for truth, wisdom, and understanding will ultimately bring you the happiness that the creator intended us to posses forever. Remember that we are actually spiritual beings going through a human experience. Not the other way around, we will ultimately return back to the spiritual beings from whence we came. There is one secret truth about life ...and that is ...**that you will never make it out alive!** If that is so then we need to live it on our own terms and to its

Make It Happen

fullest! You can play it safe and work 20 years and retire and then get another job and work another 20 years and get 2 retirement checks (plus social security) and live a safe life, but guess what, you'll die anyway... I never heard of anyone on their death bed wishing that they worked one more day. They always think of the things that they never did or tried to do when they see the end is near . It's been said "don't die with your music still inside of you" . Everything that you could ever want or need to fulfill God's purpose for you is within your reach and already inside of you. It is in your local library, it's on the computer or at Barnes and Nobles, and it's there and always has been, you just need to reach for it!

      Remember that dreams don't hit you head on- they come silently from the back Dreams whisper in your ears... always. Dreams and your purpose are that thing that won't seem to go away, it always tugs at you and although I can't explain it with words...it's always there, it exists in the back of our minds and you can never get rid of it. Welcome it, embrace it!

Miguel Sanchez

I interviewed a Real Estate entrepreneur by the name of Lynn Wardley. Lynn Started in the real Estate industry in his 20's as a Realtor in the state of Utah. As he sold houses he realized that training that was being giving at the agency where he worked was sub-par, so he saw a need for nurturing new agents and found others that felt the same way so he started his own company. He developed a training program for Realtors by knocking on doors of For Sale By owners and was aggressive at it. He made a decision early on that he wanted to build a great company. He started with 1 office -at the height of his Company he grew to 28 offices 12 of which were in Denver. He grew those offices in a State(Utah) whose total population was between 1.7- 2 million people . In some areas of the state he had over 50% market share. He told a reporter one time that he had a burning desire to do what he did. He picked great people to help him run the business .He had visualized what he wanted .He told me that he had to " get up in the morning with the desire to out do his competition. He told his agents that in order to sell Real Estate "you have to put yourself in front of Buyers and sellers" and that when someone thinks of real estate

Make It Happen

they should think of you- and when you achieve that in large numbers —something magical happens. By committing to simple philosophies and daily rituals -He had acquired over 1,800 agents and eventually sold his business (in 30 days) for Millions. By teaching realtors a simple process for selling houses -Lynn Wardley found success and his purpose by solving a problem that he felt was a problem. It can be just as simple as that...... Lynn Wardley Made it happen!

Miguel Sanchez

Make It Happen

Chapter 3

Turn Off the TV!!

One might ask why I would dedicate an entire chapter to the subject of just turning off the T.V. I felt as though this subject has become more prevalent in achieving our goals than almost any other distraction of this century other than the internet. Our time on this earth is finite, what you do with every moment that you exist on this planet matters. According to the A.C. Neilson Company the average American watches T.V. 34 hours a week! Over a lifetime expectancy of 65 years that equates to 13 years of watching television!Its even higher when you break it down by ethnicity, Imagine not doing anything **at all,** for 13 years! Imagine what small consistent personal development habits you could develop in 13 years, or if you traded the 34 hours a week for productive activities that moved you toward your purpose during that time...

    One of the things I enjoy most is watching the TV .I mean I wish there was a job that I could get paid just to

Miguel Sanchez

sit in front of the Television and watch it all day long because I love watching it. It puts me in sort of an entertainment coma. I'm in a trance, it's my drug of choice, and it takes me away from reality and projects me into a life full of beautiful people with exciting lifestyles and adventures. But guess what ... it's not reality, not even a realty show is reality...it's just entertainment. The industry itself makes billions of Dollars because so many of us are addicted to this **"Visual Heroin"**. That's right I said Heroin and I put it in bold for a reason. A drug robs you of you; it takes you away from what is real and places you in a place that is unreal. So- when you come down from the drug and you're no longer subjected to its influences, At that point you are faced with the reality of whom and what you really are and what your life is really like (which is different from that of the drug). Therefore you want more of it, and in fact the drug is really part of the problem of why your life isn't the way that you'd like it to be. You see someone who is truly addicted to something is controlled by it and their life reflects it by being by-product of that control. If you have a gambling problem you make excuses. You may gamble your bill money or even your rent or Mortgage money (when you really have it bad) and regret it after you've lost all your money. Because of your addiction you suffer the consequences of that addiction. With gambling you might lose your car, your jewelry, or even your house. **With Television you lose the life that you could have had** for yourself because you are constantly bombarding yourself with the drug of what someone else wants or says you should be, look like, do or act like, instead of the other way around.

How can we create the family(or lifestyle for that matter) that we want or should have if someone else outside of our own family is telling us what our family is suppose to be or do? I recently read that Barak and Michelle Obama don't allow Sasha or Malia to watch TV during the week at all. Why do you think that is? Do you think that the Obama Family has reached a level of success that you or I would love to have. And if the Obama's are truly a role model of what a successful family should be, then doesn't success leave footprints

Miguel Sanchez

that anyone of us can follow to achieve the same results to some degree.

The fact is that millions of people are addicted to this drug and the first step to recovery is admitting that you are an addict. I admit it. I'm an addict. So why is TV so bad for us again? Simply put- in order to have some of the things you want in life- you're going to have to do some things you've never done before to get them. Those things are typically going to be uncomfortable. That includes turning off the T.V. I'm not saying to cut it out completely and go cold turkey...otherwise you'll be right back at it again and forget about everything that I want you to realize. So let's wean ourselves off of it in small doses at first. The truth is that the time you spend watching TV is the time that you're going to need to start creating that life you want, to have those things you want to have, that house, that car, those clothes, that family, that relationship with God or a significant other or all of the above.

If your routine is to get up in the morning and take the kids to school then go to work , come home, do

Make It Happen

homework, cook and then watch TV then we're going to have to do something a little different in there somewhere in order to slowly bring this ship about 180 degrees and head in the direction that leads you to the shore of the promised land. Yes the Promised Land does exist. There's a few of people living on it and there's plenty of room left for a lot more. Think of it like this, all the people living in the Promised Land are living in Connecticut (which quite a few of them really are), but the entire rest of the United States is vacant. All you have to do is get here and you can live wherever you want in any size house that you want in whatever State that you want. But you're over in Africa and you're lost, because you keep going from South Africa to Morocco. Up and down back and forth . The problem is that you don't understand why you can't get to America. You see other people with their huge Houses and Lamborghini's but you just can't get hold of any map that can get you off of one continent and on to another. Until you ask somebody how they got to Connecticut they said "First I turned off the T.V." I remember asking a person, who was extremely wealthy, how do you become rich? In one sentence he told me

Miguel Sanchez

"just don't do what poor people do"! It took me 20 years to be able to understand the depth of that one statement. In order to get the things you want, you can't do what other people do who are not obtaining the results you want. You have to do the exact opposite of what they do to get what you want. How powerful is that!

As Human beings we are creatures of habit. Think of habits as if you were wearing a groove in your mind over and over again. That groove tends to become easier and easier to go through the deeper the grove. We tend to do the same things over and over again and they become part of whom and what we are. I recently had a friend call me and tell me that he and his wife saw someone who looked just like me. They wore the same type of clothing that I like to wear (which is usually sweat suits on the weekends), they did this like me and they did that like me. But what really struck me is that they said that he even put his money away in his pocket like me. What struck me about that was that I didn't even know or realize that there was a certain way that I put my money in my pocket, but I guess that I did and also the fact that someone else knew me well enough to even notice that I had a particular way of doing it. So in fact our habits can be so subtle that even **we** don't even realize that we're doing them. Another subtle example is for instance when I brush my teeth in the morning I somehow always start at the upper left hand corner of my mouth-every time! I put my keys in the same place all the time! Getting the picture?   But the good news is that we can change them (good or bad) and we can do it almost immediately.

Turning off the TV allows you to take the time, to put into whatever it is that you want to do, or become, or have or all of the above. Some of you might say that "I don't know what I want". There's an old saying that basically states that people can have whatever they want, the problem is that they just don't know what they want. What turning off the TV does is give you the opportunity to search your mind heart and soul to find out what it is that you truly want. First of all in order to wean yourself off of it, you might start by catching yourself when you're actually making the move to reach for the remote. When you reach for the remote you need to replace that habit with a new habit. You want to replace (eventually) all bad habits with good ones.

If you are willing to and committed to making a change in your life then you have to start thinking about what you think about. We'll get more into that later.

Use Former TV time to work on your success track

When you start to realize or understand that TV is literally killing you, not really you, but it kills the life you want, then you can start to create the subtle change that you can use to start heading to the promised land. Just knowing that you are headed to the New World (Connecticut) and are on course to get there in a realistic reasonable amount of time, can sometimes be motivation enough to keep you on track. But for those of you who are as stubborn as I am, it's going to take a lot more than just turning off the TV to get you where you want to go.

One of the things that I want to accomplish in this book is to give you immediate courses of action to take,

Make It Happen

and I do mean immediate! A lot of self developement books will pump you up and make you feel good about yourself and tell you how special you are (which you are) but fall short of giving you specific examples of what you need to do when you wake up in the morning or when you put this book down for the evening. I want to be able to help you take immediate steps today!

Some of you may be in a situation where you are broke right now and you want the answer as to how to not be broke any more. Well the simple answer to that is, to go get a job! If you have a job already (and you're still broke) then the answer is to go get a better one! The truth is that whatever situation that you're in right now (good or bad) didn't happen to you overnight. There's an old saying that "wherever you are right now, like it or not, you made an appointment to be there a long time ago".

At one point in my life I lived in a one bedroom house. I had lost my job, my cars' transmission was locked up so it could not move and I didn't have the money to fix it. My lights were cut off, the gas was cut

Miguel Sanchez

off, the telephone and the water too. On top of it all I had no food, only a bottle of warm water in the refrigerator(that wasn't working because the electricity was off), I was sick and my car got repossessed! I didn't have 85 cents to catch the bus so I had to hitch hike to a homeless shelter to get something to eat! At that very moment I was at rock bottom, but just like I said – I had made an appointment to get there long before that ever happened to me. Eventually I pulled myself up by my bootstraps, finished my Bachelors' Degree and my maters Degree, and opened up one of the largest Minority owned Mortgage Banking firms in the U.S. Co-owned a theme restaurant along with several other ventures. The last salary at a job that I had was $114,000 per Year plus bonuses. That's a long way from not having 85 cents.(today I don't have a job and I make a great deal more than 114,000.00)

It takes a little time to be broke…not a whole lot …but a little. So if you want not be broke then it's going to take a little time to get out. So if you're looking for this book as an answer as to how do I get my lights turned back on tomorrow - legally- then you might as well go see if you can get your money back from

Make It Happen

wherever you got this book from. The situation you're in is a direct result of decisions that you've made (or didn't make) long before you started reading this book. However I can help you devise a mindset and a plan to help you never have a poverty mindset (there's a difference from being broke) ever again! The mere fact that you have an interest in reading this information is the start of making the changes you need to make, in order to "Make it Happen"! We make things happen because of our desire to create or from some sort of necessity that may exist that cause us to want to change. The 3 things that motivate people are

1) Self-Preservation
2) Sexual Contact
3) Financial and Social Power

This book was created from2 of the three . It all starts with a decision... Oliver Wendell Holmes said "A Man's mind once stretched by a new idea, never regains its original dimensions".

So -back to the TV. The reason I want you to turn it off is because -like they say in Church -"The Devil is a Liar"! The TV is not your friend. When you come home and turn it on it comes from a habit that you've developed long ago. Believe me it is not by accident. The people that run this industry have long since realized the power that the TV has on our culture and on the entire world. But if you ever want to break free of the power that they have developed over you and give that power back to yourself...then you've got to turn it off! Once you turn it off it will seem a little awkward (who am I kidding, it's going to be real awkward!) But you have to take it one day at a time.

Now once you have the TV off it's time to develop your life. There's another old saying that "what you do between 9-AM-5PM is to make a living, what you do after 5PM is to make a life". All of those examples of successful people that I talked about earlier all have the same 24 hours in a day that you do. No one has 23 hours nor does anyone have 25 hours in a day. It's what you do with your 24 hours that makes a difference. Yes I realize that Michael Jackson was blessed with certain talents that only he has ...but so do you. You are just as much a child of

Make It Happen

an infinite intelligence as anyone else; we are all just blessed with different attributes. It's how you use those attributes within the time allotted to you while on this earth that makes all the difference. There's something very unique about you also. There are things that people have told you about yourself that is different from other people, that you have a certain gift or talent that they don't. You yourself may find that you're able to do something easier than other people aren't able to...well that is your gift. Believe me as I'm writing this I am going through exactly what I'm telling you to do. During the time that the TV is off is where we're going to start and how you will begin to find your gift. This is the time that we're going to find out what that purpose is and how to tap into it. Once we find our purpose or for lack of a better term our "passion" then we can move forward and start to formulate a plan to" realize our dreams" which we will get to later.

I have always noticed in my own life that when

Miguel Sanchez

I challenged myself or did something out of the ordinary that that is when I truly made some sort of progress. A simple example is someone that is working and going to school at the same time. That is a wonderful thing (I did it myself) and it certainly is not at all an easy thing to do. If it were easy then everybody would be doing it. But here's the thing, what do you do if you finished school and your working and your still broke? That's the question! Or you may be still in school and feel like quitting because it's taking so long. When you are going to school and working it takes up your entire day...you're a busy person. But then you finish and get a job and are working for a while and get to the point that you feel as though you've reached a barrier somehow that you just don't seem to be able to cross. You see I believe that what successful people have either figured out (that the rest of us haven't) is that you have to raise our tolerance level. By that I mean your tolerance level for pain and sacrifice. To me successful people have a natural tendency or ability (if you want to call it that) to endure pain a little longer than most of us; let's take

Make It Happen

a Surgeon for example. To become a Surgeon you need 4 years of undergraduate study, preferably with an extreme concentration in the sciences and then 4 years of Medical School along with another 3 years to specialize as a surgeon, then once all that's through you'll need another 3 years of residency(depending on the type of surgeon you wish to become). That's 14 years of being broke after high school not to mention somewhere in the neighborhood of 300- 500 thousand dollars in student loan debt (if your parents don't have it like that)! So who wants to be broke for 14 years knowing from the beginning that they're going to be broke that long! Believe you me ...I wouldn't want to do it either. But guess what...how many years have you been broke already??? The difference is that successful people have figured out that if you want those things you want...at some point in time you're going to have to pay a price for them. And it's either pay me now or pay me later...which one do you want? What a lot of us have not done is paid the price that we need to pay in order to achieve the level of success we so desperately want. A lot of us are just not as fortunate (so we think) to be able to make that long of a commitment or are even willing to. But there isn't one person on this earth that can't look back on and say "I wish I would have done this or that differently". We've all made mistakes but what we have to realize is that those mistakes are necessary and that success is a by-products of those learning experiences. No one has ever just gone straight to the top without making one mistake...ever. You have to make mistakes so you can learn what not to do. Thomas Edison failed thousands of times before he found the correct way to invent the light bulb. He finally figured out that by passing an electrical charge through a filament while in a vacuum caused the filament to stay lit because of a lack of oxygen. Just don't keep making the same mistake over and over again...that's insanity.

Because we have our daily routine and lives now and we didn't or weren't able to pay the price earlier in our lives, we are stuck with doing what that young person was doing...working and going to school. I don't necessarily mean that going back to

Make It Happen

school will solve all your problems. But what I do mean is that what that young person was ultimately doing was using the free time that he or she had to systematically move them from one level to another level. For whatever reason a person decides to go to College they do so because they typically want more for their lives. The people who just go to get an Associate Degree (and that's all they want) have a different tolerance levelof tolerance or expectancy than the person who wants there Bachelors' Degree. And those that want their P.H.D have a different tolerance level than those who just want their Master's and so on. So what is your tolerance level? This tolerance level or "the ability to endure pain" and sacrifice for long periods of time is in direct correlation with the level of success that one achieves in his or her life. You may want and feel you deserve the good life ...but are you really willing to give up the time, energy, commitment and focus it takes to get it. If so TURN OFF THE T.V.!

Miguel Sanchez

Chapter 4

What does it take to achieve success?

Fred Smith once said, "I listened to Bob Richards, the Olympic gold medalist, interview younger Olympian winners of the gold medal. He asked them, 'what did you do when you began to hurt"? Fred Smith pointed out that none of the Gold medal winners were surprised by the question. They expected pain and they had a plan for dealing with it. Bob Richards said "You never win the gold without hurting". To achieve the ultimate in what you yourself are capable of, you're going to have to feel some pain. You'll have to learn how to push yourself to it and through it.

One day when I was in basic training in the Army we were made to go on what is called a "forced ruck march". We had M16 rifles, a ruck sack (the Army's' version of a back pack) and weights in our ruck sack to simulate combat circumstances. We went through the woods, across streams, up hills, down hills on dirt roads, for miles and miles. Almost to the point of exhaustion

Miguel Sanchez

the Drill Sergeant yelled "Double Time " (which means to start running) as we were going up a hill. At that moment I began to see red, blue and yellow circles, and suddenly the Drill Sergeant yelled "Halt"! At the time I didn't realize it but I had gotten to the point where I was about to faint! The point of this story is that, had I never been pushed by that Drill Sergeant to the point of exhaustion, I never would have known what my limit was. At that moment I realized that I had never pushed myself to my limit. I had to have someone else do it for me, but it made me realize that I could go much farther than I ever believed I was able to go on my own. I was capable of so much more, and so are you! The Army was just the first organization that exposed me to myself. But you won't need to necessarily go into the Military to realize your full potential.

    At some point in our life every single one of us faces a challenge that might at the time seem insurmountable. It is a time when every resource you have ever had is put to the test. It is a time when life is -for just some unexplained reason -is just unfair. It is a time when our values, our patience, our compassion, our emotions, our ability to persist and continue are

Make It Happen

pushed to their limits and beyond. This experience for some people can destroy them. For other individuals it is an opportunity to become greater than what they were before they had this experience. The good news is that you and you alone have the ability to make the choice as to which one of these things you are going to allow to happen to you. It is completely up to you. Les Brown always says that "if you fall down make sure that you're looking up, because if you can look up you can get up"! History is replete with examples of people who have overcome major obstacles in their life. Actor James Earl Jones developed a stuttering problem as a teenager. Famous athlete O.J. Simpson had rickets as a child. Michael Jordan couldn't make his basketball team as a junior in High School .Motivational speaker Les Brown was labeled mentally retarded at 12 years old and repeated the 5th and 8th grades and is now a world famous motivational speaker. A.G. Gatson said "There is a way to provide against the onslaught of poverty. It is the recognition of the power of the mind". The difference that makes the difference exists completely in the way that you interpret your circumstances. Success is a mindset- **PERIOD**. It is how we communicate to

Miguel Sanchez

ourselves as to what is going on in our life that makes the difference in the actions we take. I myself have had a great deal of challenges in my life that I've had to overcome. At one point in my life I parked my car in my garage and closed the door and let the engine run to try and commit suicide. It was a phone call that I got from a friend of mine that he was on his way over that stop me from killing myself. I knew then that it was God at that very moment letting me know that he was with me and that he had a greater plan for my life and that it was not time for me to leave this earth....

Months before this incident, I had lost my job and had no way of returning to the industry that I had known for the last 15 years. Not only that I was faced with not being able to obtain another job because I was charged with a felony. The only way that I was going to create an Income was to become self employed and create it on my own...there was no going back. I had been incarcerated for 5 days and suffered what I thought at the time was a heart attack while in jail. I was so distraught that I was sent from the jail to the hospital and was admitted. I had never been admitted to a hospital in my life. I actually suffered another attack

Make It Happen

while in custody in the hospital (handcuffed to a bed) and thought that I was going to leave this earth in shackles with no one knowing where I was. After being released I suffered humiliation and depression and knew not where to turn. I was completely distraught and devastated. I was being accused of crimes I didn't commit and there was nothing I could do(I felt) to recoup my good name and reputation. I drained my savings and my 401k to pay my Attorney and as the case began to drag itself out I began to have thoughts of suicide. The pain of having to endure poverty, as well as the inability to regain my station in life was overwhelming to me to say the least. How would I be able to get another job if I couldn't pass a background check? How was I going to eat? What would my friends and family think of me? The pain was so great that my thinking process made me believe that it would be better to end my life than to continue to endure a life of pain. I thought that even if I made it through this period in my life that what difference would it make? I felt that success was only for a chosen few and that somehow I wasn't one of the chosen...no matter what I did or tried it wasn't going to make a bit of difference because

Miguel Sanchez

success wasn't meant for me. Every time that I had attempted to achieve some sort of success there was always some obstacle or thing that kept me from achieving it so why continue to try... the world would still go on without me and my life would have made no difference so why not end my life and the pain also? I found out that a celebrity died from taking 9 sleeping pills...so I kept 10 in a pile on my night stand just so when I was able to produce the courage to do so that they would be readily available. I even wrote the suicide note to include phone numbers of people whom I wanted my family to contact to know that I was dead.

    Although this might not have been a situation that other people may have interpreted as life ending, the fact was that in my own mind it was. That's the point-because I interpreted this situation to be so grave I felt that the only solution was to end my life and that there couldn't possibly be anything greater "beyond this life of wrath and pain". But little do we know that with every adversity there is an equal seed of greater or equal benefit- but you have to realize - know and understand that as a universal law. You see "we don't know what we don't know". Therefore my ability or

Make It Happen

inability to interpret what was happening to me, was a direct reflection on the action, that I would need to take, as a result of that adversity. In other words, little did I know, I needed to go through this excruciating pain in order to grow into something I'd never been before.

So one night I came home and decided to end my life and I took about a half a bottle of prescription sleeping pills. Somehow, miraculously, I didn't die that night. After I took the pills my heart began to pound and I could feel the blood rushing through my veins. I began to get very scared and thought to go into the bathroom and try to force myself to regurgitate. Instead I laid back down and prepared my mind to meet my maker. No one knew that I had attempted to take my own life...well until now. The next day I woke up sick and very dehydrated. The one thought that kept me going through my mind in my attempt is that in trying to alleviate my pain I would just be passing it on to those that I loved and that loved me. I couldn't bear the thought of the pain and anguish that my mother would endure if she had to bury a second son and last child that both had committed suicide. But somehow my life was spared, (or I just didn't take enough pills) to stop my heart from beating. I'll tell you what happened after that later....

Everyone wants a better quality of life, even a person trying to commit suicide believes that their life would be better being over. The question is you willing to pay the price of obtaining it. Some of us may want a better physical body than we have right now – but are you willing to go to the gym to get it? In order to achieve the success we want -the garnering of it will not come from the getting of things- but from a change from within.

The example that was used in one of the former paragraphs of the student working and going to school full time is an example of what it takes to achieve success. Once we have reached a level that we are typically comfortable with we tend to settle into that place. There's another old saying" that the road to success is filled with many tempting parking spaces", this is true on so many levels. While working in the post secondary education business I noticed that students would come to these schools based on moving away from a painful situation. They usually have reached a point in their lives where they are forced to make a decision-because the pain of their lives at the present moment has forced them into a corner. You see out of necessity the student decides to take action because that particular day their lights got cut off or something happened to make them take action. The problem is, that it took some type of catastrophe in order for that person to do something about their situation instead of "digging the well **before** you get thirsty" .That student is pushing themselves - in the beginning- just to become a productive member of society. But what if we pushed ourselves without having to wait until a catastrophe takes place? Once we get that job or promotion how often do we continue to push ourselves to higher heights? Successful people do consistently what unsuccessful people only do occasionally. I'll elaborate how I got from rock bottom to making 6 figures a month later....

    In your daily routine I realize that you have to work to make ends meet. But have you really broken down your day to figure out where your time goes? What do you do before you go to work? What do you do after

Miguel Sanchez

you come from work? If you normally get up at 6:30 A.M., how about trying to get up at 5:00? Yes I know that is difficult...but remember what we're trying to accomplish here. We are trying to adopt successful habits that can move you to the next level. During this extra hour and a -half that you've just created for yourself we're going to (as T.D. Jakes would say)" Maximize the moment". For the first 15 minutes we're going to find that quiet place. I don't care if it's the bathroom, a closet, or the garage...but find a place, even if it's outside, that you can have some silence. During this time I want you to meditate. I want you to focus in on your breathing and empty your mind and go inside of yourself. At first it will be difficult. At first your mind will be cluttered with all types of junk, worry, bills, things you have to do and so on. Just remain calm and peaceful and try to listen for "your source ". You see when you were born no one gave your parents or you an owner's Manual on "How to operate this child and turn him/ her into the perfect person". No one gave us a book and said this is exactly what to say to this child and this is what you need to do and when you are finished with all of these instructions that ...you will have the

perfect Human Being. The only thing close to telling us exactly what to do with, to, and for each other is the Bible, (or the Quran, or whichever you prefer). So the reason we are spending this extra time in the morning is to get closer to that source that you come from. And believe you me , that source is so very real...the sooner you realize the power that God has the sooner you will begin to make that trip to the promised
land(Connecticut).

    What we are doing during this time is drawing into ourselves and creating a connection, a bond if you will ,that helps give us the strength to persevere and endure (if you don't realize you're going to need it, then realize it now). I don't think that there is one personal development book or motivational book that doesn't mention or recognize this power. This book is no exception. God is everything, and everything is God. Without tapping into the spirit and the power of the Almighty, true success will never be reached. You can have all the money in the world and still not be happy. I know that people say that all the time ...and

Miguel Sanchez

most of us just want to have the opportunity to find that out for ourselves! Believe me, when you start making money it just makes you more of what you already are. If you're a drunk when you get rich, then you just buy more expensive alcohol, if you're generous before you become rich then you will be even more generous. Once you have money and buy the house(s) and the car(s) and the jewelry and take the fabulous vacation(s) you will soon realize that there is nothing in a diamond bracelet or under the hood of a car that can satisfy that inner craving that we were built with that satisfies you spiritually. To me we are all spiritual beings that are, for the moment going through a "Human Experience". And when we pass we will return to our spiritual forms once again, that is why material things can never completely satisfy us. So this journey to become who and what you want to be begins inside. It is through making that connection with God that you will begin to truly see what and who you are and why you are here and what you must do while you are here. That's why we need to get up earlier in the morning, because if I told you to do it in the evening then most of you would have 40 million excuses as to why you couldn't do that. And by the way

Make It Happen

"*excuses are tools of incompetence used to build monuments of nothingness, and those who exercise their uses are seldom capable of anything else*" I don't know who said that quote but I thought it was about time that we kind of got excuses out of the way. Try to start with about 15 minutes. I know that doesn't seem to be a long time but believe me when you first start it will seem like forever. So start slow and try to concentrate without interuption. When I say without interruption. Don't get up to go to the bathroom, don't go check on the kids, and don't move. Just stay as quiet and as still as you possibly can. You've heard of "Peace be Still" well this is it!

I know that you want to ask the other question of what were you supposed to do with the other hour and twenty minutes. That's your workout time. Yes you need to work out. Some of you who are reading this are already 1 step ahead on this one. I have been working out since 1987 (that's when I joined the Army) and ever since then I have done some sort of consistent exercise regimen. There's plenty of information about

Miguel Sanchez

what working out can do for you. But for the purpose of your own success, a workout routine is going to be key to your endurance, your appearance and it will most definitely help you to feel better about yourself. If you're going to be able to increase your tolerance level (as we discussed earlier as to why successful people are successful) then you have to have the endurance to be able to do it. Once again , this is something that may not be as easy thing for a lot of you, but the key is to stay focused on all the reasons why you're doing all of this in the first place. After enduring my hitting rock bottom – connecting with my source was the first step back to succeed on a level I had never dreamed of.

What does it take to be successful? It's going to take every bit of your focus you can muster in your body .With every ounce of every fiber that you have in you, you have to be committed 100%! Successful people are relentless!

One of my first experiences with my ability to accomplish something I put my mind to came while I was in the seventh grade. I was in Military school (not because I was bad) and it was my first year there. The school was for young boys from 3rd grade to 8th

Make It Happen

grade. All the officers were in 8th grade. In order to become an officer you had to be appointed as an officer at the end the seventh grade and come back the next year as an officer. It wasn't long before I realized that for some reason or another I didn't like people who were my own age telling me what to do. It's hard to listen to someone who is 12 when you're 11...What I also figured out was that the other boys there felt the same way also. Because the other boys didn't like it either so they would constantly get into trouble and get demerits. So at the age of 11 I thought to myself-what do I need to do in order not to be told what to do and become one of the ones who tell other people what to do? My answer to myself was, that all I needed to do, was to do whatever I was told to do, when I was told to do it, with no back talk and do it to the best of my ability. By the end of the school year I was told that I was not only going to become an officer the next year in eighth grade but I was going to become a company commander. That meant that I was going to be in charge of other officers also! For the first time in my life I set a goal for myself, focused in on the activity I needed to focus in on to accomplish that goal and before I even realized it I had

Miguel Sanchez

achieved my goal! I actually was chosen long before the school year was over .it was an unprecedented accomplishment in the history of the school because officers were usually appointed from the boys who had been there since the third grade. I did it in one school year, I was given the responsibility, as an officer, to be in charge of other officers along with 120 other cadets after only a few month of attending the school! The point of the story is that I focused...at 11years old. At the end of my 8th grade year I was promoted to cadet Captain – the 2nd highest rank in the entire Academy.If I can do it at 11 you can do it at whatever age you are! It boils down to something very; very simple...I just made a decision ...that's it. It's not rocket science, but it does take effort, and consistent commitment, so much so that after a while you don't even realize that you're even doing it.

Think to yourself, have you ever put your all into something and it turned out really well ? Have you ever done something that you were proud of doing? It takes willpower to accomplish something great. If you've ever done it before then that automatically gives you a blueprint of what it takes to do it again and again! By

Make It Happen

the way- when you start to have that little voice in your head tell you the negative things in your life then switch the channel and remember those good things that made you proud of you.

Here's the kicker, if you fail at it, then be thankful for it! Failure just means you're that much closer to your dream because you've just figured out how **not** to do something! One of my biggest failures was at a time that I was attempting to go into the promotions business. I partnered with another promoter in order to do an exotic male dancer show! There was another club in town that was doing it every week and making about $30,000 per week doing it. I was so proud of myself for overcoming so many obstacles I had to overcome in order to make the show happen. We flew the dancers in from Miami and had a line around the corner. However my partner had placed flyers inside the competitions venue a few days before the show and the owner of the competitors' club sent the police to our show and had it shut down because we didn't have the proper permits to do the show. We refunded the money and I lost $23,000.00 (which at the time was a lot of

Miguel Sanchez

money to me). After I thought about it I realized that promoting strip shows, was not what God had intended for me to use my talent of perseverance for had I listened. At that time I did not have the connection to my source as I do now. My source was speaking to me loud and clear at the time but because I didn't listen – I suffered consequences which I need not to. I just wish he could have let me know about $23,000 sooner!

What we've surmised in this chapter is that success takes relentless commitment and focus. Connecting with your source ,changing what you do in the morning, altering your schedule is only the beginning of what it takes to MAKE IT HAPPEN! Let's begin to break down what happens after you start making these changes , inevitably people start to drift back into old patterns of behavior , the next chapter helps you to stay on point and how to turn the steering wheel back in the direction you want to go.

Chapter Five

How to get Motivated ...and Stay that way!

The way I see it is that a lot of self help books will try mainly to focus in on what gifts you have and the potential that you have within (yourself) to be able to succeed. The problem is that once you go to a motivational seminar or read an inspirational book or message you get motivated **for the moment**. What then?? How do we keep ourselves motivated on a consistent basis so that day in and day out we stay on that ship that is sailing to the Promised Land (Connecticut)? It's hard to stay motivated every single day! Think if people only went to work when they felt like it! The DMV would never be open! Who wants to go to the DMV and stand in line or wait for hours? Most of us make that New Years' resolution to lose weight or change this or that and by February or March we're back at the same old routine and we've lost our oomph or vigor. Actually 85% of all New Years' resolutions are

Miguel Sanchez

over by January 15th. I see it every year at the gym. At the end of December and all through January, there are all types of new faces in the Gym. It's crowded and you can hardly find a treadmill. But by March, it's back to seeing the same die hard gym rats that stay there all year round. So the question is how can we make **every day** January 1st? Did you know you are free to do that? We can make everyday Christmas if we put our mind to it!

Well in my mind there are several ways to accomplish this task. Any one or combination of these "triggers" can and will work. Pick one or several but pick it and let's go to work!

However before we go there as promised, I want to give you some things that will help jump start you and put you back on your purpose track. These are things that you can do within 24 hours that can help you shake things up, break up the monotony, and help you to re-focus on what you want so that you can get back on track again!

- Buy a motivational/self-improvement book (hopefully another book of Mine) I'll have another one for you to read!)

Make It Happen

- Listen to a motivational speech on youtube
- Go to church
- Pack up your things and go stay in a homeless shelter –tonight!
- Read proverbs in the Bible
- Fast for at least 24 hours and think about your purpose whenever you feel hungry
- Find a quiet spot and pray immediately
- Call someone that you trust and can talk to and share with them that you have lost your focus
- Go back and read some of the things that you may have highlighted in this book already
- Go for a walk in a peaceful place
- Go workout

Set a goal -for yourself that is very hard to reach (but not impossible). By obtaining the goal you start to believe that you are capable of doing what you put your mind to achieving. And then repeat it. When your conscious mind creates a vivid picture of what it is that you want, your sub-conscious mind has no choice but to believe it. As a matter of fact your subconscious mind believes whatever you tell it...repeatedly. So tell your-self repeatedly what you intend on doing or having. Say it out loud, say it before you go to bed, and say it when you wake up in the morning! But say it...and then say it again and again! I know you've heard this before ...that's exactly why I'm saying it again-because it works!

Remind yourself of what you don't want-By this I mean that realizing some person, place or thing that you don't want can be a huge motivator. Most people can and will tell you that focusing in on something negative will not give you results. I'm here to dispel that rumor. I started working out when one day I got out of the shower and I had a picture of my Uncle on my bed (forgive me Uncle). What I started noticing was that the shape of my body had the beginnings of taking on the exact same dimensions as his body. In short I was beginning to look just like him! However he had a huge belly, little legs, and not to mention a bald spot (I just shaved my head completely to get past that one!).But at that moment I was determined **not** to look

Make It Happen

like my Uncle. (And just to set the record straight my Uncle lost a huge amount of weight and eventually became slim and trim). I knew that if I continued to follow the same eating habits and not taking care of myself then that was eventually where I was headed. Now I know that when this book gets published it may cause a family scandal. But again I'm letting it all out so that I can not only give self -imposed therapy but to help you as well. So in fact not wanting something- and staying focused on what could happen if you don't - can be a very powerful motivator.

Focus on revenge-Marcus Aurelius said " The best revenge is to be unlike him who performed the injury". Success can be a very powerful form of revenge. I know this one will seem a bit off to some people but this is one of the most powerful motivators I've seen. And I don't mean revenge in a disruptive violent way but what I do mean is that success can be achieved by just focusing on all the (as the young people say)" haters" out there that told you "I told you so " or you can't or won't be successful. Think of their faces when you they see you driving past them in your brand new Bentley

Miguel Sanchez

Drop top with tags that say " HWULKME" or "NOW I C", or even better... "PAID 4"! You don't necessarily want to rub it in their face (cause I know that's what I would want to do) but knowing that they know ...is good enough! So when you have to get up in the morning and go work out ...think about that guy that you liked but he didn't like you because you were a little overweight or that girl who wouldn't talk to you because you didn't have any money.(I once had a girlfriend that broke up with me because she said I was too poor) Of course these are shallow individuals to begin with but they can be used to your advantage if negative reinforcement motivates you. Believe me, you will face your biggest opposition when you are closest to your biggest accomplishment!

Focus in on what you do want-This one is pretty obvious- but so many people don't dream enough. You know, some people may call me a little odd, but anytime I'm near the ocean, I'm drawn to it. I have to go and see it. I will go out of my way to be near, close to, smell it and revel in it. I cannot for the life of me tell you what inside of me draws me to it but I will just sit on the beach for hours (if I have the time) and just

Make It Happen

draw from its beauty and power. There is something very mystical about the ocean. To this day I feel that we have yet to discover what the ocean has to offer mankind. But one thing that I know is that I ultimately want to live right on the ocean. Not by the ocean, not near the ocean...but on the ocean. So I go there to imagine what my house will look like. What beach will it be on? I imagine myself and my significant other walking out of the house and taking long walks down the beach while the cook is cooking (a healthy) breakfast for us. I focus on the lifestyle that I want so that I do not deviate from those things that will ultimately lead me to that lifestyle. No matter who you are, where you live or even what country you live in. all of us on this planet have one goal and one goal only...that goal is..." to be able to wake up in the morning and do whatever it is that you want to do"... Period. There's absolutely nothing wrong with focusing in on those things that you want. Although they will never completely satisfy you the way that "God" can they can be an exceptional means of motivation.

Miguel Sanchez

Focus in on God-This one is the crème-de-la-crème. Any one of these motivators can and will work as motivators to drive you on a consistent basis. However focusing in on your spirituality can change you forever. Not only can it be the motivating force behind achieving in life whatever it is you want to achieve but this can change your character as well. I could (and some people have already) write an entire book on how becoming more spiritually connected can change your life. When I lived in Atlanta I was opening up a restaurant called "Hip Hop Cafe". We opened it and it had 51 televisions. Almost every individual in the restaurant had their own individual TV; we also had Hip Hop memorabilia all around the walls in display cases autographed by the actual artist themselves. We had Memorabilia signed by Lisa "left Eye" Lopez, Biggie Smalls , Tupac ,Big Pun and many more. We played Hip Hop videos on the TV's and served drinks named after artists. I met artists like Outkast, Ludicrous, Warren G. 8 ball and MJD, Swiss Beatz to name a few. But during the time we were putting this restaurant together I began praying and praying hard that it would come together. To connect this altogether- One day I was driving along HWY 20

Make It Happen

and I saw a girl in the back seat of a car all dressed up as if she were going to church. I decided that I would go to Church that day and I would follow that car and go to whatever church they were going to. I followed them to a small Church but their Church had a gravel parking lot (and I wouldn't drive my brand new BMW on gravel) so I went across the street. By the time I walked out I was Baptized and saved! Do you think that was an accident? You see all the time I was praying I was asking God to come into my life. At the time I had no Idea that he knew exactly how he was going to do it. Since that day I have understood and developed a relationship with God so much so, that even as I write these sentences I can feel his power coming through my mind down my shoulders on to my arms and through my fingertips to this keyboard. That is how I know that we have such an awesome God! And I believe that he wants everyone to have everything they want in life. But the way is through him. Trust me on this one. Go to Church, Temple, Synagogue, Mosque... or wherever you have to go to get to him, but get to him, because the same God is in each of these places but he has to reach us through different channels but they all lead to him.

Miguel Sanchez

6) **Focus in on a person you care about**-One of the reasons I chose to write this book is for my Mother. I wanted to make her proud of me. I know she would say" son I'm already proud of you". But to me that's not enough. I want to make her so proud that when she walks down the street people want **her** autograph just because she's my mother. She has dedicated her entire life to her children. My brother committed suicide in 1993 at the age of 23 over an argument with a girlfriend. He did it to prove to her how much he loved her, which again substantiates my point that you can love someone else so much that you would do almost anything for them. Why not devote the success of your life to them or for them. I don't mean take your own life but to endorse your life by complimenting theirs with your success. Especially since the motivation of my Mothers' life has been to the life of her child. What better way to thank them than to reward them in becoming even more then they could ever have dreamed of for you. Right now as I write this we have soldiers in Afghanistan (they are gone now) . All of our soldiers get a check on the first and the fifteenth of every month. They're being paid to go to war. There are people over there that are

Make It Happen

standing in front of a building and blowing themselves up for free! Meaning that people are willing to die for what they believe in. Their motivations may be very obscure but it is no doubt to this entire world that what they believe in has changed how we go through airports, the street in front of the White house and many other ways we have led our lives. No matter how backward we believe their ideals and cause is to us, in their mind they are finding ways to stay motivated. How do you convince Terrorists to do what they do? Do they think they will ever be able to adopt the principles on which they are fighting for? How in the world did Bin Laden keep people living on the run in the dessert for years at a time with no end in sight? Now that's some motivation!! And by the way... I believe that we had the wrong people looking for Bin Laden. All we have to do is have Bin Laden miss a couple of child support payments... believe me child support would've found him a lot faster!!!!

Focus on one day- at-a-time- As I'm writing this I think to myself "how am I going to continue to write this"? What do I write next? Well each journey

Miguel Sanchez

starts with the first step and if you have to eat this elephant one bite at a time then that's what you have to do. For some people to be motivated they have to do it day by day. So start with today...and I mean ***today***. "Procrastination is one of those character flaws that people put off trying to correct". By breaking down your goal or plan one day at a time it doesn't seem as overwhelming. Just make ***today*** a success. Just do the things that you have set forth for yourself to do that inch you along the path to where you want to go.
Its fine to have days off for your goal but those days should be pre-planned an ordained as specific days to do whatever you heart desires. Even if it's lying in the bed all day. But on your "success track" days you need to be on point. Maybe Monday -Friday are your success track days, maybe Friday through Tuesday. It doesn't matter what the days are... just that they are. When you make them- stick to them. Let me say that again-stick to them. That's the purpose of concentrating on this day-by-day. When that alarm goes off at 5:00 in the morning or whatever time it goes off, you'll either do one of two things. You'll jump up and be excited about the change you're trying to make in your life or you'll ask yourself

Make It Happen

"what am I doing this for again"? Your attitude each day will determine your altitude at the end of your days. Someone once said that the way you do anything is the way you'll do everything". After about 3-4 weeks it starts to get harder. Again there goes that tolerance level. You can't forget that successful people endure...they keep going...they take the pain and take it again...and they press on. Not that successful people like pain any more than you or I do . But they have realized if you allow yourself to go through a limited consistent amount of pain it can result in a lifetime of luxury and contentment. That's why they have a bigger house than you...get it, got it, good. If not becoming all you can possibly become is not a goal for you then you can stop reading now and gift this book to someone who wants more in their life. So maybe you use a combination of focusing in on God - one-day at a time and what you want ultimately. Whatever the combination you use it has to be enough that when you use it causes you not to roll back over and put the covers back over your head and say "I'm not feeling it today" ...You have to be able to plant that picture of whatever that person place or thing is in your head. For me when it comes to working out I think about my Uncle and I jump up (Sorry Uncle). For you it could be the fear of having to buy a whole new set of clothes because you have to go up one dress size. Whatever that thing is, it is your "trigger" and for some of you may have to pull it every day, some every 3 days ...whatever you have to do, have your trigger ready to go at a moment's notice. These are 6 "triggers that I have just given you that you can utilize to force you into action. There are infinitely more that you can use or any combination of these that are going to be key to you succeeding. This is really worth repeating. Finding an internal trigger is what is going to pull you day after day after day.

The Trigger you don't want to use

The trigger you don't want to use- however it can be very effective - that is the last straw. When you get so tired of some condition, person, place or thing that you just can't take it anymore, that's when you make a change. It's extremely coercive, but because different people have different tolerance levels, it can be extremely damaging. It's the same reason why some women (and even some men) stay in physically abusive relationships. A lot of people I've heard in conversations ask "how could she let him do that to her"? Well, you're not them and they're not you. We all have different breaking points. The real point that I want you to see is that you don't have to let it get that far. See it before it happens(dig the well before you get thirsty) and use this text as a guide book to keep referring back to, to get some sort of inspiration not to have to learn the hard way. Like I've done and like some of us keep having to do. All of these thoughts were already inside me. Why would I have to wait for someone to hire me and fire me in 2 days to begin to realize that I finally should be attempting to do what was in me all along. Don't wait until you get beat down before you decide to come up, choose to come up before you get beat down!

The fact is that this "trigger" exists in each one of us right now. Think about it, are you where you want to be? If you're not where you want to be or at least aggressively headed to exactly where you want to go then that trigger hasn't been activated yet. And I don't mean where you want to be in a place where you aren't supposed to be at in the first place. What I mean by that is that if you're working for the State and you're trying to get a promotion in a job that isn't or wasn't meant for you then you're wasting time in achieving what God really has in store for you. Why would you be wasting your time at a call center when you secretly want to be a Fashion Designer or a Singer or Dancer? The truth probably is, is that you were able to get the job in the first place and it pays the bills for now until you can do better later. The problem is that later turns out to be much later and the next thing you know you're too old or have lost the enthusiasm to chase your dream. Now you've got kids, and bills and all that other stuff that life throws at you to keep you from finding you and really living a prosperous dream life. But the fact of the matter is, is that you still can have the life you really, really want. You just need to know how to go get it realistically. You can easily get comfortable in a life that you have carved out for yourself and your family. For many of us as long as the bills get paid "on time" and you can go on a vacation every once in a while then we're satisfied. But

Make It Happen

is that it? Like Al Pacino said in the movie Scarface "Is this what it's really all about Manny"? Even after Scarface got all the money he could ever of dream of having he still wasn't satisfied ...that's because of that spiritual thing I was speaking about earlier. But when we're talking about someone who has a normal existence, are we really at that place you want to be yet. Do you feel you are there? What would you do if you knew that you could not fail? Would you be an Actor, a Ballerina, a Football or basketball player? Would you be an Astronaut, or painter? How about an Interior Decorator or Doctor? If you have that desire to be something other than what you are right now then typically we haven't reached the tolerance level it takes to ignite that trigger you don't want to ignite. Think about this, if you were to ask someone who was old and in the hospital and about to die what they thought about, they usually don't respond with their loving memories. They would tell you about the things that they never got the chance to do. How, after all these years, they really wanted to go skydiving but never took the time out to go. How they loved to cook and wish they had tried their hand at opening up a catering business or restaurant.

Miguel Sanchez

One thing I know they wouldn't say is that "I wish I would have worked one more day"! So those of you who are those mid-level Managers putting in 10,12, and 14+ hours a day trying to be good "Company Men/Women"- which there's nothing wrong with that if that is what you ultimately want- but don't let the effort of trying to put your all into something , but it keeps you from giving some to yourself.

I thoroughly believe in the "Law of Success" by Napoleon Hill, which by the way I highly recommend going out and getting (after you finish reading my book of course!). One of those principles is to basically give more than what is expected of you. When people see that you work hard at whatever it is that you do they tend to draw towards you. It just is what it is. Everybody wants a good deal and if people can get more than what they think that they're paying for, then they will draw to it every time. When I was young there was no such thing as a Dollar Store. Now they're everywhere. Why do you think that is so...value is why...

But getting back to the point of the trigger that you don't want to use: People get comfortable in their everyday lives and once they've reached an altitude of

Make It Happen

comfort ability they tend to lose that hunger or thirst for what could truly be possible or what could be. Why is that? Why do we get to a place and seem to coast? Tony Robbins says that "people tend to gravitate away from pain and towards pleasure? And if that's the case why didn't that Women leave the first time her husband smacked the bejesus out of her? My thought again is tolerance level. So what if that same Woman who allowed that man to physically abuse her for years, could she take that same tolerance for pain and put it into staying up late at night studying? Could she go to the Gym and work out so that the next time he tried it she could do like J-Lo did in that movie "Enough". (See I told you I liked TV.) Successful people have re-wired their thinking process. They think differently from the rest of us. When a successful person becomes comfortable, they force themselves into becoming uncomfortable. What I mean by that is that a successful person has sort of an obsession to become successful. I'm not saying that you have to become obsessive but you do have to develop a trigger that allows you **not** to get too comfortable. The moment that a successful person feels as though they're beginning to coast, they

Miguel Sanchez

think of or create some type of new goal or challenge for themselves. It can be conscious or subconscious...but it exists. I once had an ex-girlfriend like that. But it wasn't to achieve anything; it was the need for Drama. If everything was going fine, then that wouldn't satisfy her, she had to create Drama in her life to keep her going. You and I know at least one of these types of people. (They're usually in our family). Jerry Springer has become wealthy by making a living for over 20 years exploiting these folks! So how can we manufacture or duplicate this same sense of urgency or need to achieve in our own lives to get exactly what we want and desire to fulfill ourselves.

Chapter Six

Breaking the cycle of Mediocrity

OK so far we've discussed triggers that you can use to focus in on in order to create that sense of urgency to do what you have to do every single day to reach that place you want to be. So far we have you getting up an hour and a half each day to give yourself more time during the day to help accomplish what you want to accomplish. Now during that extra hour and a half that we have manufactured, we've discussed utilizing that time for meditation and exercise. I know some of you are saying "you lost me at exercise" but this is when we have to allow those triggers to kick in. What about that person that said you wouldn't be anything , or what about doing it for that person that you love so much, or what it would feel like going over to your old High School buddies house in that Drop Top Bentley? Well this is how it's going to happen. That is the purpose of the trigger to begin with.

Miguel Sanchez

So now you've meditated and you've gone to the gym (reluctantly) and you're on your way to work. Here is one of the differences of the way I see things and the way others view them. I want to give you more of a step by step approach to success. For instance when you get back from the gym take a shower, put on your clothes and get into the car. I want you to put either my CD or some other motivational/ inspirational speakers CD and listen as you drive to work. So that means turn off the radio. Yes that's right, the radio is **"Audio Heroin"** not to be taken. Once again we are using every minute of our time to produce a better you. Don't worry you'll get down time from all of this but for right now follow the yellow brick road that will take us to the Promised Land. You see I want you to squeeze out every minute of every possible day to be able to become and have more of what you want for you. Because you know what…it's all about you. Think of how your children's future would be if you could provide them with every possible thing they could ever want. Think of being able to pay cash for them to go to whatever school would accept them! Again this is the use of triggers when you think to yourself "I really don't feel like doing this". Then think again of that reason that you are where you are is because you haven't been doing some of these things (consistently over time)! It goes right back to tolerance and what successful people are willing to sacrifice and the pain that they're willing to endure. Why would you allow yourself to keep dealing with that Boss you can't stand rather than put some effort into what it takes to get away from that boss forever?

Now that we're on the subject of work and that boss that you can't stand. We're going to talk about what you need to do while you're at work. What we're going to do is do the absolute best job that we can do that day and each and every day (I told you success does not come easy). I guess you may ask me why are you having me put all this effort into a job that I eventually want to leave anyway. Once again, it's not for them, it's for you silly! Everyone knows that Martin Luther King said that "if you're going to be a garbage man, then be the best garbage man you can be". He was using a Law of Success that I spoke about earlier, but even more so than that I want you to start forming successful habits. This is absolutely essential. Forming

Miguel Sanchez

the habit of giving all that you have to give- even when you don't want to- is an essential characteristic that is common place amongst those that have achieved something greater than the average individual. It's simply because they've done more than the average individual. This trait is no exception to the rule. I don't care what it is that you eventually want to be or do there's going to be some aspect of it that you don't necessarily like. Maybe Oprah Loves the interview part but she hates going to meetings to decide who the guests are going to be. Or maybe she doesn't particularly care or having to sit still while production people put on her make-up. But then again what woman doesn't enjoy someone else pampering them? Whatever the case may be...we want to prepare and train ourselves to be the best that we can possibly be...no matter what the task. It was the Army that taught me (amongst other things) to get up every day and exercise. Because of that training I will have a workout regimen for the rest of my life. Because I was able to see the benefits of adopting certain habits that gave me long term success I was able to incorporate them into the fabric of me. There are infinite habits that you can start

Make It Happen

today and make today January 1st - so trust me when I tell you that when you leave the job today and every day you want to know that you've given them 110%. Not for them but to become a better you.

    Now you've left work and you would normally be tired but you still have some energy left because now that you've been working out you have more endurance. Now it's time to go home and start working on you. This should be the happiest part of your day. This is your time. This is where the bulk of everything that you need to do is going to get done, and this is where you make your life happen! Once again it's important that you get the workout done in the morning rather than the evening. So stick to the plan. Now I know that many of us have school age children and that this is where soccer practices and homework and cooking Dinner and all of that comes into play during those evening hours. But this is the most crucial time for your personal development. You see here's where we separate the girls from the Women or the Men from the boys. Most of us do those evening duties then watch TV and go to bed. Isn't that true? Well this is where we go over beyond and above. If you want to have that thing you want so badly, then you have to do something that the people who have what you want were willing to do that you haven't been doing for all this time.

Alright, this is no different than what a lot of people have said before and I will be no different. I want you to sit down and write down these things that you want. I mean everything from possessions to where you want to be financially. I want you to be specific. For instance don't say that you want to be rich. How rich do you want to be ...exactly? Put a definitive number on it so that the realization of reaching that specific number, goal or thing is tangible. I once read that the actor Jim Carey, before he became the Jim Carey he is today, wrote himself out a check for 10 million dollars and told himself – I believe it was ten years- that he would be able to cash it. And it actually happened in a little under his goal! Having a tangible goal is oh so powerful. So in your first couple of evenings I want you to (don't try and stretch it out to a month) expand it and refine it. Put time limits on yourself. Say that I want this amount of money by this day in this month of that year. I want to have this kind of relationship by this day of this month of this year...or I want this house with this square footage with this color carpet and these color drapes with this many Big screens and so on...

Step 2- Figure out what we really want to do or become- When I say figure out what we want to do or become I mean what you would do for free. I'm talking about if you would enjoy getting paid for sitting home watching TV then that's what you would put down as your goal. Benjamin Franklin once said "The constitution doesn't guarantee happiness ,only the pursuit of happiness-it's your job to catch up with it", so I hope sitting at home watching T.V. is not your true purpose , but I'm just trying to get a point across as to not putting any limits on yourself or your capabilities. If you want to be an actor or a TV anchor or whatever it is write it down. Think of those triggers if you're hesitant about putting in the effort to do this. One thing I think about is that my Aunt passed away recently. As she was dying which was about a week's process, the only people to come see her were 2 of her neighbors, her 2 boys (my cousins) and my mother (her sister) and me. My Aunt has a brother (that same Uncle I told you about earlier), but he did not come. But that was it. Her obituary was about 2 or 3 sentences. Basically that she was born on this day had 2 boys, some grand kids and great grand kids. That's it. She was cremated and only her 2 sons were there for that. I had another Aunt that passed away from cancer and it was the largest funeral that I'd have ever personally attended. There were hundreds of people there. Even that same Uncle showed up for her funeral. What was the difference between these two women? They both new each other almost all of their lives, but what could have been the difference in one being celebrated so abundantly and the other people barely knowing that she even existed? What will your funeral be like? Who will come to give their respects to you when you die? The difference between them was that one was full of life, she enjoyed life and people enjoyed being around her...she made them laugh. The other was a miser; she rarely worked a day in her life and mostly lived off the state for most of her life. She could be mean at times and at one point in her life was a raging alcoholic. (Like I said my family may disown me) however I loved both of them equally but if you are reading this book what would your obituary say if you were to write it today? You see if you can figure out who you are and what you're purpose is for being here and then take action on that purpose, then you become pleasing to God and would have fulfilled your destiny. And for the fulfilling of your destiny God rewards you with a truly blessed life. So write down what you want! Use that quality time that you have to create a better you!

Step 3- If you don't know exactly what it is that you want it's o.k. but it's not o.k. , o.k.! You may have to read supplemental material to help you figure out what your purpose is. I suggest" the purpose Driven life". If you're having a hard time with it still then just read on and hopefully I will be able to give you some sort of hint or path to pursue to help you in your quest. Finding it though is not always the easiest thing to do that's why God gave you a whole lifetime to figure it out. Now some successful people have been able to figure it out very quickly. I saw an interview with "Drake" the rapper and the interviewer asked him who he was and what he does. He answered with his name and then he said "I do what God put me here on earth to do". He was 20 at

Miguel Sanchez

the time of the interview. Obviously he'd found his purpose very early in life ...and some of us aren't so lucky. Don't worry ..."every flower doesn't blossom at the same time". But what you need to do is start (if you haven't already) figuring out what is that you do. Believe me you don't have to be great to start, but you need to start in order to be great. Start with writing down things that you like to do in your spare time, things that you just do to be doing. Start there, if you do them anyway then those are the things that you would do for free. God leaves clues to what it is that you should be doing...some obvious and some not so obvious. Think back and think about compliments people have given you over the years as to something that you've done well. Or maybe you already know what it is but think that it's impossible for you to pursue it. Well if you're reading this and your 75 and really wish you could be in the NFL, it probably ain't going to happen. But if you're 23 and think you have it, and then the next step is to make a plan on how to go for it. So let's make a plan. In order to make this plan you need to start at the end instead of the beginning. You need to figure out where you want to end up at so that you know where to begin.

Make It Happen

Remember the list of things that you want, we want to incorporate those things in our plan.

So let's say you want to live on a house on the beach in San Diego and wake up every morning looking out over the ocean. You want a Bentley Drop Top, BMW 650i, White Range Rover, and a Phantom Rolls Royce to name a few. Now, you've got to work your way backwards from here. (Keep in mind that I'm not being nearly as specific as you need to be on your wish list). And let's say that my dream occupation is to be a business owner. Let's say a restaurant owner. But at the present time I work for a Bank in the accounting Department. How do I get from one place to the other? Right now you have a net worth of $0.00, bad credit, a car note (and not that nice of a car), 2 kids, a dog, and 5 credit cards that you're paying the minimum payment on. Wow, seems like a lot right? Well welcome to America. A Federal Reserve study says that about 43% of Americans spend more they earn actually about $1.22 for every dollar that they earn. The average American has about 7 credit cards including 1 debit card. So I guess you're not alone. So the Phantom Rolls Royce seems so impossible to get and that the future doesn't look as though that it will ever happen. In fact you've probably given up on the idea at all that a restaurant may even bee in the cards for you. It seems like it will take forever to get from here to there. Well don't fret Miguel is here to help you. I had a restaurant myself (and believe you me its hard work!)

So the plan needs to go from the bank, to the restaurant, to the beach. So let's put it together!

Every winner has scars. In order to win you need a spirit of non-conformity. So your plan has to be one of non-conformity. No great plan ever was accomplished without testing its planner to the limits of his/her determination or faith. But it is so hard to see what might be possible when you're in the trenches of trying to make something happen. You must trust in yourself, and in God. That it will happen. I didn't say might happen I said will. That's part of the plan ...knowing that what you want to be will be.

So now back to the beach house. To have the beach house you have to determine how big it's going to be , where it's going to be , what price range its' going

Make It Happen

to be and so on. Being specific is tantamount to reaching your goal. If the Beach house is going to be 5 million then you're probably going to need to have more than 1 restaurant or you may need a chain or at least more than one location. To get more than 1 location you need to be successful with the concept in one location first and foremost. To get the successful 1 restaurant you need a sub-plan for that. To get that plan you need to know how to put a business plan together for a successful restaurant chain...or maybe be able to buy an existing chain that has a proven track record. To get that you need to have the down payment and the credit to buy it. To get the down payment you need to borrow or save the money. To save the money you need to have more income coming in than you do going out. To do that you need to examine your finances. To do that you need to sit down at the kitchen table and figure out where every dime goes that you spend every month. If you don't have a kitchen table it's going to take a long time to get to the beach house. What is really being done here (since I know you've figured this out already) is that we're backing into our success by figuring it out from the end to the beginning. The plan itself is the easy

Miguel Sanchez

part. Implementing the plan is where most of us get stuck. Why is that? If I just drew a road map (well sort of) to get you right where you want to go , then what's the problem with following it? This is what I have been trying to figure out for years. I just finished speaking to someone who felt they were overweight, which is no different from millions of Americans. Now they are probably 30 pounds or so over their ideal weight which is not too terribly difficult (depending on how you look at it) to remove. There are all kinds of ways to get rid of that weight. I myself have had an issue with my weight. I have talked to all kinds of people about how to lose weight and they gave me all kinds of diets. I even tried one where you have coffee toast and a grapefruit (and that's it) for a week and your guaranteed to lose 10 pounds. I lasted about three hours. Then one day in the gym a trainer explained to me (in a way that I could understand) the actual way that the body processes food. What it does with it and what it keeps and what it discards. Once I understood why things were the way they were I was able to lose 30 pounds over a three month period of time. Now the difference was that I understood exactly what I needed to eat and that I felt comfortable in eating it every day. I could basically design my own meals. But I was able to understand why I was doing it and what it was doing when I did it. That is the same way your plan has to work for you.

We need to be able to break down the mechanics of your plan so that you can actually see what is happening each day. Once I discovered that the body didn't store protein but it definitely stored sugar and carbohydrates then I just started eating protein. Now a lot of people have heard of protein diets, but the difference with me was that I understood why I was only eating protein. Body builders were telling me about eating 6 times a day and measuring your food and having protein shakes. If you're like me there's no way I can just stop in the middle of a meeting and say "excuse me it's 10:00 A.M. I need to step out of this meeting and go eat 2 boiled eggs and a tuna fish sandwich. Eating every 2 or 3 hours would help you to speed up your metabolism and would certainly help you to become leaner. But what I knew that I could and would do, is reach in the refrigerator and grab a chicken leg and keep it moving! That I could do! I can eat chicken all day any day. It may not be something that you want or are able to do but it worked for me. One thing is for certain, I'm not measuring a cup of brown rice and all that, but if my goal is to become a body builder then its what I must do to achieve the results I want . As a matter of fact one of the body builders told me I can only have so many grams of something. I told him that I didn't have a triple beam scale at home (I think only drug dealers have those), so that wouldn't work for me. So we both can lose weight, we just have to find the right path that we are willing to stick to and abide by ,that we will go down in order to end up at the Promised Land. We all can get there, some by boat, some by plane, some by Camel...but we all can do it!

If you know that part of your plan involves being able to save a little each month so that you can have the down payment for the restaurant and you're not in the position to save then your choices are simple. Spend less or make more...which path works best for you...or you could do both (that's a little tougher but it works faster). The choice is yours. So when you come home in the evening time your first thing that you have to do is take care of the household and the kids and so on...but

Make It Happen

after that it's that kitchen table to figure out these expenses and where they are going. Once you do that you can figure out which path you're going to take to be able to save the money. If you're a single parent it may take taking on a roommate, but I'm sure that thought probably already crossed your mind and you don't want to do that because you don't want just anybody around your kids. So that leaves you with other options. Moving to a cheaper place. Well you thought about that too and you don't like the neighborhoods or the schools for your kids in the cheaper areas. So then there's option 3 which is to make more money. One tactic that I've seen people use when they need money immediately is that they go into their HR and increase the amount of dependents on their w-4's so that they get less taxes taken out. Although I don't suggest that you do that it's a gray area and you need to be aware of the tax implications that you can be liable for at the end of the year . However you can offset that by owning a business (we'll touch on that later). But the point is these are all an immediate fix to a much needed money crunch. But remember it didn't take 1 trip to HR to get you into this situation so it's definitely going to take more than that to get you out. You have to have an extended plan to get you out permanently so this situation never ever happens to you again.

    So the true plan is to have a long term plan that will get you exactly what you want and place you exactly where you want to be. You want to think of exactly what you want your life to be like in a specific amount of time. It's important that you assign a specific amount of time in order to measure milestones on the way to getting there. When you think of the way that you would like your life to be you also want to make sure not to put any limitations to it. Dream big! The only limitations that we really have are the ones we place on ourselves. So don't hold back no matter how outlandish you may think it is. The reason is, is that when you truly know what it is that you want you will develop the drive and motivation to make that thing happen, as long as you want it bad enough and are willing to do what it takes to get it . As a matter of fact that last sentence was success in a nutshell. We have to establish that dream first and then work our way backward from there. As you work your way backwards and figure what it took to get you there, you can start to put your plan in place. By doing this you simplify the decision making process in the future because whatever doesn't coincide with your ultimate goal then it is definitely not the way to go...hence decision making 101 becomes very standard.

Step -4 Take Action! Napoleon Bonaparte once said "Men take only their needs into consideration, never their abilities". So add up your abilities...those things that you find to come easily to you and not so much to others. Write those things down. Let me repeat that, **WRITE THOSE THINGS DOWN!** While I'm in the mood to use quotes let me also use another one that may fit at this juncture written by Catherine Pulsifer (an Author of Inspirational Words of Wisdom) said ... " a determined person will do more with a pen and paper, than a lazy person will accomplish with a personal computer." So don't be lazy about what you want. After all it's all about what **you** want -not what I want. When I say don't be lazy about it (your goal) I mean that with all sincerity. I'm telling you this out of pure experience, because I have suffered so long with the disease of being , what I feel is" mediocre", that it has prompted me to write these pages and to stop dragging my own

Miguel Sanchez

feet to be able to live comfortably . But at times I can drift into other things that are not pertinent to the overall goal in life. The overall goal is and always will be "to wake up in the morning and do whatever it is that we want to do". To do that we must take some sort of concentrated focused action for a period of time so that that action relinquishes all the results you ultimately want to achieve. As I've said in different ways over and over again, it is how long you are willing to endure the pain of that action in order to endure the pleasure of its result

Chapter Seven

The Spiritual Side of Success

There are 2 words that are commanded by God in the Bible more than any other command. The 2 words are fear not!

Without a doubt this is the most abstract and integral part of this book. You can market your business, knock on doors, achieve multiple degrees, or any number of accomplishments-however it is only God that gives the increase. You can plant seeds all day long but it is God that brings the sun and the rain in order for your crops to grow.

When you are in harmony with what you are destined to do you **will**

Absolutely know it without a doubt. The very first time I gave a seminar that I created- I gave at my own home. I started on a Friday evening and talked for almost four hours. I had everyone come

Miguel Sanchez

back the next morning and spoke again for an additional 7 hours. I and the participants loved every minute of it ! I was on a roll and everyone gave me raving reviews! What I had was a revelation-an epiphany if you will. After it was over I had to take 2 Aspirins because my knees were killing me for having stood for such a long time. But what I realized, was that while I was talking I felt no pain whatsoever. I was in a zone and in my element. It was like a light bulb went off in my head that affirmed once and for all that I was doing exactly what I was put on this planet to do. Not only did I have a spiritual connection but I had an epiphany about my sense of completion. That it isn't about how much money I made -but my currency would come from the amount of people I served. Your purpose will in some way coincide with service to others in some shape or form. I figured out that the effect that you have on people is really your true currency. What is it that people need that your talent can provide?

Make It Happen

Remember that your talent cannot be learned-it can only be discovered.

    I felt that somehow I needed to be able to communicate to as many people that I possibly could –that you can have the same experience-if you chose to. When you are doing what you were meant to do you can lose track of time and yourself. When you're doing what you're meant to do then time has no meaning to you. You're focused and consumed with that thing you do. You have to realize that when this happens you have found -your purpose. That is how we have been created and that is God's way of communicating to you that this is what your journey here on earth is to be focused on. To do any other activity that that does not have to do with that purpose is just a distraction meant only to deny you the time that you could be living a life of happiness, peace and prosperity. It's as simple as that. In order to have this experience you have to understand the spiritual side of how God, faith, belief and things that are intangible- work.

This chapter alone could be an entire book in and of itself (and actually it has been). Understand this-that the entity that was able to create everything that exists has limitless power that we are in no way able to fully comprehend. Imagine for just a moment the sun in the sky. How could it possibly stay burning all of these millions of years? Have you ever known anything that could burn for that length of time-ever? Why does it never burn out? What possible power could have created something so powerful? An entity that has the capability to create something that powerful, has the capability to create a being that has limitless possibilities also- makes sense? The only limits that you or I have have been placed on us by ourselves. Someone once said —"that I have seen the enemy ...and it is us".. God has the physical (or metaphysical) capabilities for conveyance of resources that we won't be able to fully comprehend in our lifetime. He has the control of a limitless amount of resources that he and only he can direct toward you at his will. The question is how you align yourself to receive those resources either on request or as consistently as possible. How can we harness the power of God? If you are the greatest creation of the creator whom created everything then why would he not create a way for you to create whatever you wanted in your own life? The point of all of this is that you absolutely have no limitations whatsoever! If there are no limits then why don't all of us succeed? When you understand the connection that you have between yourself and the creator as well as to one another you will begin to understand how much power each of us truly harness.

In the bible everyone knows of the story when Peter and the Disciples were in a small boat crossing the sea of Galilee when a tremendous storm came over them. As the storm got worst and worst, they saw a figure approaching the boat that appeared to be Jesus walking on water. Of the 12 disciples, only one got out of the boat and with the help of Jesus was able to walk on water. The first clue is that if you do choose to "make it Happen" you're definitely going to have to get out of the boat and trust Jesus. Peter not only recognized the voice of Jesus but he was obedient to God. The other 11 Disciples stayed in the boat.

If you think about it -the internet was here in the year 1492 when Columbus sailed the ocean blue! Cars existed in the 1500's. Airplanes existed during the time when Jesus walked the earth. The table of elements hasn't changed as far as I know during any of these historical times. In other words steel and Iron and all of the elements that it took to create all of these things I mentioned existed during all of these dates in history. The point is that we had not evolved enough to realize what existed and what it took to combine these elements to create an iphone, a jet, the space shuttle and so on. The universe is full of endless possibilities that we still have yet to discover. And if the universe is full of endless possibilities and so then are you also! The same fact exists today. There are inventions that will amaze us that will be placed in the mind of some child that hasn't been born yet . Right now there is a ship that is being developed that will go from New York To Los Angeles in 12 minutes! You probably say that's impossible – but I bet Christopher Columbus would have said the same thing if you would have told him that one day humans would fly in a steel capsule going 400mph while seated having an alcoholic beverage! God created us so that anything is possible; we just haven't realized it yet!

In order to Make it happen, it is absolutely imperative that you have a spiritual relationship with God. Because God is the one that created everything on this planet, it only makes sense, and is absolutely necessary that you (on your journey) are connected to that source of power. The stronger your bond with your source, the quicker you will reach your destiny. Why is that you might ask? Because that source has all the answers! God will speak to you if you talk to him. One of the ways that I know to ask God to reveal himself to me is to ask him for a sign. It is something that only he and I know what the sign is. I ask him to show me the sign 3 times so that I know it is him speaking to me. One time he gave me the sign 5 times! I'll give you an example. One time I had a job offer to move from Atlanta, to Phoenix. In order to know whether this was the right move for me I asked God to tell me that that was where he wanted me to go. I asked him to tell me by giving me

Miguel Sanchez

a sign that had the word Phoenix in it. Two days later I was driving and I happened to look up and there was a sign that said University of Phoenix. The next day my current Boss (who at that time would usually go to Costa Mesa ,California for conferences) came to my office and said that she would be out of the office because she had to go to a conference in Phoenix. The next day I had a conversation with someone who just ,out of the blue, had no idea that I was considering a job in Phoenix and mentioned Phoenix to me. After that there were 2 more signs. Bottom line is that I listened to God and moved to Phoenix. As it turned out it was one of the worst jobs I ever had. It was not a good fit for me at all and I only stayed there a year (because I had contractual obligations). However after leaving that job I was able to land a new job in Sacramento, that was one of the best jobs I ever had in my life. I met some of the most wonderful people you would ever want to meet at that job. It's almost like God was moving things around sort of like the colored blocks in a rubix cube in order to put things in place so that I could get to where I was supposed to be, but I had to wait a year to get there. That is how God works, you may not understand why

Make It Happen

you would ask God specifically for something and he puts you in one of the worst positions you could be in only to bless you later. I had a hard time with it at the time but believing in a power greater than yourself and being grounded in that belief helps to guide you in your decision making even when it seems that you may have made the wrong decision. They say that God works in mysterious ways. While I was in Phoenix I found a church home that I absolutely loved! Do you think that it was by accident that God would put me in a city far away from anybody and everybody I knew and a job I hated but gave me a spiritual connection greater than the one I just left? Funny how that works! You've got to have that connection in order to understand what is going on in your life (at all times) so that you remain patient and diligent in your pursuit. Without that spiritual connection you can be blown around like the wind. Some of you reading this will get it immediately but there may be some that will not be totally convinced. Put it this way-if you haven't been able to "Make it Happen" in your life like you want to (and I do mean in all facets), then what could it hurt to try it God's way? Make the connection, form a relationship with God, pray

Miguel Sanchez

often, think about God throughout your day-talk to him- don't worry, he'll talk back...

When I moved to Las Vegas-I had $86.00 in my Bank account.. I felt humiliated –and I had strayed away from my former close relationship with God. I struggled tremendously. A year later I was still struggling. I sat in a room and stayed utterly depressed because of my fall from making a six-figure income to not having the ability to put gas in my car. At one point in time I got a minimum wage job that was at a laundry facility for the casinos in Vegas. I would sort dirty wet sheets (sometimes with urine, blood, vomit etc..) ,pillow cases, washcloths and so on, with all the foul smells that go along with dirty laundry. It would take 2 weeks of-the hardest physical labor I had ever done- to make $400.00. I knew that I had to do something to change my situation. The only option I was left with was to pray. As I began to form a greater relationship with God I began to change the way I saw things. I took Real Estate classes and prayed that I could get my license (remember I had a Felony) and I received a it. I quit my job and had faith and started surging in Real Estate. I monetized videos on "You tube" to make money and

Make It Happen

created a website so that people could book me for speaking engagements. I used money to invest in Real Estate and began my climb back...Today I am extremely successful but it never would have taken place without that connection/relationship I have with God. It was God that gave me the direction and helped to correct my mindset and the way I perceived my circumstances that helped me to change the direction that I was headed. By connecting with him I was able to "transform myself by the renewing of my mind". He was the one who connected me to the right people with the right advice. He was the one who gave me the energy and mind set to read all of the books I needed to read to put content on"You Tube". God is the one who gave me the words to put in this book that will hopefully touch millions of you! Think about this-We may not get along with or connect to everyone –which is normal. Somehow some way ...God connects to everyone ! He reaches all of us in some way shape or form. If he is in each one of us then we are all interconnected. When someone finds that thing in them that seems to reach all of us then they not only have found their purpose but they found that thing that God gave them that is truly to be used

Miguel Sanchez

for the service of others. When someone sells millions of books , Cd's, computers, cleaning products; whatever, they have found that connective tissue that links us all- because in essence we are all a part of the same entity. Look at it this way-if you have a product or service you want to sell in your community-and God is in every community-does it not make sense to go to God to connect to every community on this planet?

But the question I want to ask you is why you are here? What could possibly be the purpose of your existence? When I say existence I'm not necessarily speaking of your personal existence but the existence of all mankind. Why do we just have 5 senses and not 6 or 7 or even 8 for that matter? Did God put us here because he was board, and created us so that his job would be to create thoughts in humans that lead to actions that cause prayers to be answered? You may need to read that line again! What I believe is that God created us with a sense of purpose to do or accomplish something, in which we would spend a lifetime searching to find out what that thing is and simply do it. Your job on this planet is simply to become exactly whom you are supposed to be ...period. In order to find or align yourself with that purpose it is mandatory that you have a spiritual relationship with that higher source. Often we can't see clearly the path we should take or the decisions that we should make because our thought process is impaired. We rationalize our decisions based on secular principles. We do what the world tells us we should do. However when you make the connection to that higher source then your thinking process and the way that you interpret circumstances change. In other words it's not in the discovery of new landscapes that we grow, but by seeing those new landscapes with a different set of eyes that truly causes us to fulfill our destiny.

For instance, there should be no difference in who you are and what you do. The two should be one in the same .Now his job (God's that is) would be to help us find that thing and for us to help others find what their purpose is also. I even believe that while I'm writing this, that God is divinely intervening to make sure that somehow these words I write will touch some of you in ways that cause you to take some action in which he intended for you to take but needed me to write this in order for you to see it and then go for it! I know and understand that he uses us as instruments to affect one another. I believe that God is divinely orchestrating the things that happen (through the use of thought) so that our prayers can be answered. That is why prayer is so powerful. Where do you think that thoughts come from? I believe that they come directly from the source (the Father). Now be careful, because they can also come from another source ...and we all know who that is. So you ask...How will I know the difference? **Go to Church!Read the Bible!** Develop that personal connection. My Pastor delivered a sermon one Sunday that asked the question "Do you know God"? He used an analogy that many of us think we know someone like a Michael Jordan or even the president of the United States. Just because you've heard a great deal about that person or read about them or seen them on T.V. doesn't mean that you actually have a relationship with that individual .That is the message of this chapter in a nutshell. I don't care if you are Mormon, Muslim, Baptist or Wicken! Find a church, Synagogue, Temple, Mosque or whatever, in order to connect to that higher power. I also believe that because we are all so different that God communicates to us in different ways so that we might be able to understand his ways in a way that is familiar and comfortable to us. What I mean by this is simply that I believe that every religion, cult, sect, or belief in a higher power, all believe in the same God. In other words, finding God is like solving an algebraic equation...there are many ways to solve it but the answer is always the same. So if God has the ability to put a thought in your head that can have you take some sort of action, could it not be an idea that can make you rich? Could he put an idea in your head that helps the right person find a cure for Cancer, or diabetes, or Arthritis? If God can bring the dead to life, could he not give you an idea of how to solve the problem with your relationship? If Jesus can walk on water do you think he can help you find that man who actually will watch lifetime T.V. with you! By making the connection to the higher source you allow yourself to disrupt your natural tendency to use your intellect and use an alternative decision making tool by asking yourself the right questions to ascertain the correct action to take that will empower you. Instead of acting off of emotion you will use that inner source as an anchor for all important decisions.

Take for example, these "Mega Preachers" of today that preach wealth and prosperity are instruments of God but they are also instruments of secular society. They realize that they have a market and they produce and provide a product that people want and need desperately. They sell hope. They sell it with conviction and with continuity that boggles the mind. Some of these "Men (and Women) of God are worth Millions of Dollars! I believe that if Jesus were here on this earth today, that he wouldn't be driving a Bentley! Think about it like this, in Jesus' time he was capable of drawing huge audiences. Do you think he used his ability to command a market, in order to sell a product? Would Jesus try to sell his book to the crowd on the Sermon on the Mount? He had a great deal to say; couldn't he have tried to sell it? Don't get me wrong, I believe that these Preachers have excellent knowledge of the Bible and a keen eye for what their congregations' are thirsty for, but I do believe that their lifestyles do not necessarily represent the word of God. They are very simply telling you exactly what you want to hear and using specific versus and stories in the Bible to do what is essentially a motivational speech but done in Church. And because it's done in the name of God we believe that the message comes directly from him and we pay to hear it. The only problem with that is ...is that all he wants us to hear? Or is there more? Do most of us pick up the book and read it from cover to cover to really unveil the truth. Because we all know that the truth shall set you free. So if you know and read the truth will you be free? I believe that you can. I believe that there is no owners manual for humans except for the bible, Quran, Or Sanskrit, So how do you truly become free? I believe that taking the time out and reading the word of God for yourself and meditating on it will ultimately help you in your journey to success. The words of God are so powerful that people are willing to blow themselves up because of their interpretation and belief in those words. Now that's some powerful stuff that after you read it you're convinced that you and your family will be blessed if you kill yourself in the name of Allah. So be careful on how you interpret those words. I don't want anybody to read this book and then go out and blow themselves or anyone else up!

Miguel Sanchez

I once heard a female pastor tell a story about her children. She described one of her sons as an excellent Baseball player. He was bigger than other kids his age and that he had a keen sense for the game. She spoke about how he would be in tournaments and that as they played, if her sons team did well in the tournament they would have to come back and play another team either the same day or the next day or even the next game. The tournaments could last the entire weekend all the way until Sunday. One day in between winning games the family went to get something to eat and then they came back to the playing field. When the family returned back to the baseball field the Pastor noticed that her son seemed to have his head down and his shoulders were slumped just a little. She couldn't tell exactly what was going on with her son until she looked up and saw the other team that her son was playing. It was a team that annihilated her sons' team earlier in the season. The kids on the other team were bigger stronger faster and were extremely serious about their sport. They were the kind of kids that when they were born the parent put a mitt in one hand and a baseball in the other. But something strange happened. As 2 of the other teams players happened to be walking by her they were speaking about her son. They said "wasn't that the kid that hit the home run and the run who did the double play against us"? Once her son heard the 2 boys mention his name, his shoulders straightened up , he stopped slouching and in fact they had to bring him down a few notches. He got his pep in his step back and his countenance back. Well the moral of the story is that the enemy knows who you are and what you are capable of and even though he may seem more powerful than you, he knows who your father is and the power that you actually posses even when **you** may not know what gifts you have and what power you wheeled..

Read the word, and find out for yourself. Form a bond between you and God that is close and cannot be altered, manipulated, diluted, changed, or slighted in any way shape or form. Make it solid as a rock! That faith, that relationship, that belief is the purest girder of absolute success that there is on this earth. Pay close attention to this point: You are no different from the source that created you! If your source is all powerful- then so are you!

Formula(s) for success: The SH+I+D=R Formula

There are many events, problems, circumstances, and occurrences that happen to us on a regular basis that cause us to alter the course of our destiny unconsciously. It is the decisions that you make due to those circumstances that determines your ultimate destiny. This formula is a tool for you when faced with those difficult times that we are all faced with.

The formula is simply this: **S**tuff **H**appens + how you **I**nterpret (what happens to you) + what you **D**o = Will equal your **R**esults

This formula can be used and applied in any situation or circumstance. The greatest gift that we have been given as human beings is the ability to make whatever choices we want and those choices over time determine our ultimate destiny.

Another formula was derived from a Quote by Michael Novak which is simply that " The wise learn from tragedy; the foolish merely repeat it". Which when injected into a formula may look like this **E +R=W**. Meaning that **E**xperience + **R**eflection = **W**isdom.

Simply stated; that when you reflect back on your experience, that then and only then can you truly learn from that experience. Without reflection you are doomed to repeat the same mistake over and over again. Life University doesn't care how many times you take the class, it will keep giving you the same lesson over and over again until you learn it...and then you pass. Some people never get out of a class their entire life!

The ancestor of all action is a thought. If you look at the position that you're in as of this moment...it all stems from a previous thought. How much money is in your bank account? How happy is your relationship and/or marriage? How well do you perform at your job? How are you thought of at your job? What type of shape are you in? Are you proud or afraid to look at yourself naked in the mirror ☺ Are you in control of your life and your circumstances? Another formula for success is **T+E=R** **T**houghts + the **E**nergy put behind those thoughts will determine your **R**esults. Knowledge is power but enthusiasm is the power switch! Without enthusiasm then your chances of success are mediocre at best. How many people do you know that are successful at something they have no zeal or zest for? I've talked to many young people about what they want to do in their lives and what they are passionate about and a great deal of them have no clue. They have many different likes and don't really know or understand what they are passionate about...yet...How can young people narrow the list down without having to necessarily go through the experience first? I believe that part of the solution is for the parents to instill a sense of purpose in their children as they are being raised. In my family there wasn't a choice of whether or not you wanted to go to college ...it was always the question of which college you were going to choose and which one would accept you...The answers regarding purpose for young people can be answered through deliberate guidance. The ability for young people to find their purpose lies in the way that they view and perceive the world. We see the world through our own values. For example... 2 twin brothers (one who drank alcohol heavily and one who didn't drink at all) when one was asked why he drank he

Make It Happen

responded "because my Dad was an alcoholic...The other brother when asked why he didn't drink at all responded "because my Dad was an alcoholic" . We make our decisions based on the way we perceive the world through our own eyes and our own embedded value systems.

Miguel Sanchez

Chapter Eight

The Pursuit of happiness...

> "The constitution doesn't guarantee you happiness, it only guarantees you the pursuit of happiness, and your job is to catch up with it....
>
> **Ben Franklin**

Everyone deserves and is entitled to happiness. The problem is that they just don't realize it. The word happy is derived from the Icelandic word happ which means luck or chance which in the United States seems to be the status quo, but it doesn't have to be. We all want a better life, better relationships, financial prosperity, and comfort. The good news is , is that it's all possible! The true path to happiness is progression. To be in a constant state of progression and to break through that

Miguel Sanchez

barrier that is holding you back and get to the other side and find out what you are truly capable of!

The key to making it happen is taking the first step to whatever that thing is. It starts when you open your eyes up in the morning. The moment that you open your eyes you have a choice to rise up or hit the snooze button. The moment you rise you begin to make choices – the beggar and the Billionaire all have the same 24 hours in a day-it's how you use the time that makes the difference every second of every day. If you want to change what's going on in your life ,the bottom line is to start doing the things that you know you should be doing when you're supposed to be doing them. It's really that simple. The things that you need to do are exactly those things that will get you what you want-the problem is is that most of the time you're not going to want to do them. The reason for the problem is that your mind isn't wired to make you happy or wealthy –it's wired to keep you alive and to survive. Whenever your mind feels danger or that something is going to hurt you(let's say for instance exercise) then the mind kicks in and causes you to think about it and hesitate. Sometimes you feel like going to the gym and sometime you don't. The difference is that the successful person goes when they don't feel like it. The successful person makes that extra sales call even when they don't feel like it. The successful person over time starts to see the results of being consistent even when they didn't feel like being consistent.

    You have to make a Decision, then make a Commitment, and then take Action. Making a decision to change your life or having a better relationship with your significant other, or to change any part of your life that you feel falls short of where you believe it should be-is not enough to make a change. You have to make a commitment that whatever that thing is- is done. You have to make a commitment- that today- is the last day that this thing will exist. If you want to improve, or get better or you want to start a business, you have to make a commitment to start it right now, at this very moment!!!It starts with discipline to take the necessary action to make this thing happen! But remember that its this discipline of what you do hour by hour that subtly starts to make the change happen. You don't have to be the smartest person in the room to be successful-it's the one who procrastinates the least and gets things done.

Getting things done is an import ingredient in Making it happen! The moment you start achieving (even small results) is important for the mere fact that you start to gain momentum. When I go to the gym one day and skip the next 2 days and go the next day then I'm not creating momentum and I get discouraged about changing my body . The moment I get 3 or 4 days in a row going I start to gain momentum and I get enthused about keeping the consistency up. When I get 7 Days in a row going then I really get excited because I know that my record is 11 days in a row. I now have inspiration to keep pushing. It's the same thing when you want to change or get better. To hesitate is the enemy of opportunity-simply don't hesitate-just do it!I love what Jim Rohn said when he said "You can always have more than what you got because you can become more than what you are. But if you don't change who you are then you'll always have what you got"! You've got to decide if you want to be an impactful person or not. I can absolutely tell you that it won't involve sitting on the couch every day watching

Make It Happen

Jerry Springer...I can also tell you that it won't be easy-it's simple-but it's not easy. It took me years to come to the conclusion that I could no longer concede to mediocrity .I realized that I was going to have to become someone that I had never been before. It took days , weeks and months of reading every personnel development book I could get my hands on. I started listening to personnel development tapes and seminars (consistently) every day since 2012 and am still doing it right now. I committed myself to wanting to become better-to trying to figure out why others were enjoying exquisite lives and others were struggling week in and week out. I started a library of all kinds of books of leadership ,Real estate, self improvement, motivation, spiritual books, books on psychology, financing, stock trading, business and anything else I could find that could push me forward. Slowly I began to change, I began to incorporate subtle habits of working on this book a little at a time. I started putting my content together for my seminars, I formed a partnership to acquire a contract with the county to increase my cash flow. I gave blood twice a week just to be able to have different streams of income to push me closer and closer to my goal. One day I looked up and I had made 6 figures in a month...and I continue,,,

The 7 Levels of Happiness

Stage 3- Self Actualization, joy , contentment, work is play, all needs are met , spiritual alignment, long lasting nurturing relationships, deep friendships, peek health

Stage 2- Progression , signs of upward mobility, beginnings of Love, realization of passionate purpose, Giving back , helping others, philanthropy, milestones are achieved , goals are met and new ones created

Stage 1-Positive direction, traction, instillation of positive habits, goal setting, beginning of personality change, change in relationships, discipline begins, leaving comfort zone.

Ground Zero-Existing, no positive movement in either direction, working to survive, stable

Minus 1-Constant problems, financial instability, consistent worry, stress, lack of focus, lack of concentration

Make It Happen

Minus 2- deep depression, drugs, alcohol, problems attaining basic needs such as food, clothing and shelter, health deteriorates

Minus 3-Suicide

From now on when people casually ask you how you're doing you can say- well I'm about even or I'm a 1 or I'm at a minus one right now, but I'm coming up and so on...

So let's explain what these stages are :

Minus 3- Suicide- There is an interesting quote that says that "suicide is the sincerest form of self-criticism". A person that has reached this stage in their life is not so much interested in killing themselves or in dying, what they truly want to accomplish is ending the pain. They have reached a point in their life, that the pain that they're in, is so overwhelming that they can think of no other way out to alleviate it. It is a shame that living in a country with such absorbent wealth and resources that a person can find no other way to overcome their pain and anguish but to end it all in this manner. As of the writing of this book a new VA study indicates that 20 veterans are committing suicide every single day in the United States. That is a staggering amount of unnecessary hopelessness.

Minus 2- at this systemic stage a person falls into catch 22 that is extremely difficult to get out of- typically without some sort of help. Sort of like 'Pookie" (played by Chris Rock)in the Movie "New Jack City" who arose from being a drug addicted crack head into a police informant but only through the help of actor "Ice tea". The same sort of hopelessness that can trigger suicide presents itself in individuals' with addictive vices. They fall into this trap due to lack of education, upbringing, incarceration, mental health issues and a plethora of other premises. We see this every day in our society with homelessness, drug addicts and so on...It can start off with something as simple as starting to smoke cigarettes , which is a vice in and of itself but the act of doing it seems to satisfy a need to belong or to assimilate to a particular crowd. The need to alter ones state in order to attempt to temporarily escape the pain and or aggravation that one has fallen prey too, Segway's itself into potential suicide- if left unchecked and untreated.

Make It Happen

Minus -1 We have all been at this level at one point or another in our lives. It occurs quite a bit when we are in our early stages of life and are trying to establish ourselves, We can't seem to make ends meet, the power gets cut off, there's too much month at the end of the money. Somehow problems seem to overwhelm us at this stage of our lives. There's one problem after another, we can't seem to make and may or may not see a way out. You may be in a constant state of despair due to hardships; you feel stressed out and under pressure and you are constantly trying to find a solution to gravitate away from the pain.

Ground Zero- there are millions of people who exists in this plain. They go to work every day feeling unfulfilled and unappreciated. They have jobs that pay their bills and keep their heads above water but other than that are not progressing forward and that results in a lack of happiness because we need to feel as if we are progressing in a positive direction in order to gain true happiness.

Usually you will hear a voice in the back of your mind that refuses to go away that tells you that you should be doing something else. It eats at you slowly, but because you have children or a mortgage and/ or responsibilities that keep you stuck in a rut that you just can't seem to deliver yourself from. Ground Zero can also happen when you are comfortable. Comfort can be a formidable enemy to your [potential] you. The mere fact that you have all of your wants and needs met can cause you to relax and not ever seek to find your true end of the road. Someone once said that "The road to success is filled with many tempting parking spaces". That is the danger of Ground Zero.

Stage one – Is exciting and ambitious. When engaged in stage 1 one you begin to see the light of your potential .Moving to stage one can come from an epiphany or just being sick and tired of being sick and tired, at some point you began to raise your standards and your wants that can be learned through some experience or event, whatever causes you to take the necessary action to change your life and begin to go in the direction that you were meant to be going in is almost a miracle in and of itself. Keep in mind that just because you get promoted at your job and are now afford to be able to do somethings that you hadn't been able to do in the past does not necessarily mean that you have arrived at stage one if your job is not the thing that you were meant to do. Stage one truly involve heading in the direction that you are supposed to head in according to God's will and purpose for your life. Trying to modify that purpose simply by increasing your income doesn't qualify. Stage one truly involves invoking the habits and disciplines necessary for completion of your life's mission, At this stage you are beginning to realize what that mission is and start heading directly towards accomplishing it and it only. There is no deviation and you begin to become completely and utterly focused on something that you are truly passionate about, you begin to wake up happy, excited about life and its wonders. You begin to expand your creativity and meet new and interesting people. Connections start to come together, your relationships are beginning to blossom and you have a greater sense of self.

Stage Two – In my opinion this is the one of the most satisfying stages that you can exist in. when you reach an existence when you can change the lives of others because of your ability to be philanthropic. At this level you have changed your persona and have reached a level that very few ever realize. Just because you may be making money and able to give back is not completely achieving stage two status. It's a mindset- it's a discipline of the mind body and spirit that is beginning to show signs of maturity in all things- in all ways. .

Stage Three- The most difficult and virtually impossible stage to reach in life. Some call this stage self-actualization Although there are millions of people in the United States there is a small percentage of people who reach certain milestones in life, such as Medal Of Honor winners, Hall of famers, Grammy and Oscar winners, the Presidency of the United States, Senators and Governors- I could go on and on but I say this to say as a percentage of the population these are rarities/anomalies, As it is with Stage three individuals. They are people who have gone past the day to day living process and have completely dedicated their lives to nothing else but the advancement of Mankind. Like John F. Kennedy having a vision of a man walking on the moon before the knowledge of how to do so even existed. They are

Make It Happen

like the dream of Martin Luther King. We have visionaries in the 21st century that are giving away most of their fortunes like Bill and Melinda gates as well as warren Buffet. Realist see things as they are but dreamers see things as they can be – therefore all progress will depend on dreamers of Stage Bezos are examples of the kind of dreamers I'm speaking of with their recent private space flights.

We all want to be happy no matter who you are what country you live in , your social status , religion ,color , gender , race , education level, or sexual orientation- we all want it. No matter who you are, you too can Make it happen – you just need to want it bad enough and have a plan to get there and work that plan every day. As you work your plan happiness will creep up on you without your knowledge and knock on the door and eventually move in with you and never leave. We all want our children to prosper and for them to be as proud of us as we are of them.

Miguel Sanchez

Chapter Nine

Time Management – Spend it or invest it

> *"If I were given eight hours to chop down a tree, I/d spend seven of it sharpening my ax".*
>
> **Abraham Lincoln**

If each chapter of this book were to represent a part of the body that makes up an entire human being then time management would be the brain. The brain gives guidance and conscience instructions to the rest of the body. Examples of un-concious instruction would be your heart beating or your eyes blinking –these things happen without you necessarily giving instructions as to stopping and starting these functions, although I have heard of individuals slowing their heartrate through meditation. However I digress.

In order to make it happen you will have to manage your time as though it were like money. Every day you get a bank of time that you have the choice of how to spend. It is equal to 86,400 seconds every day, 168 hours a week , 8,760 hours a year . No one gets more and no one gets less. The difference in "Making it happen" will depend in a high regard as to whether or not you spend your time or invest your time.

Since we are all allotted the exact same amount of time – then the obvious difference to all success is how you invest it. I'm not going to go into deep time management theories like going to a destination and making sure you plan it so that you only make right turns.

Once you know your purpose and you're passionate about obtaining it , it's much easier to allocate your time appropriately. What you spend your time on from minute to minute depends entirely on what you believe are your priorities and what you are focused on. For instance – let's say that you are a person who rarely if ever works out. In addition to that your reason for not working out is because you say that you don't have the time to do it. However let's say for instance that I were to offer you $100,000.00 to work out for one month 5 days a week and at the end of the month you would

Make It Happen

receive the $100,000.00 as an experiment for time management, How many of you would have the money at the end of the month? Probably everyone that reads this, I'm sure. The idea here is that you make time for what you want to make time for and what is important to you. Working out now becomes important to you because of the $100,000.00 increase in monthly household income.

    Inevitably every moment of your time is spent (or invested) based on practical or emotional decisions that you choose to make. These decisions are based on your values, your self-esteem, and your character. If you believe in yourself you will inevitably believe that the things you want can be accomplished and will put in the time and effort to make them happen. If you don't believe or don't conversely have the innate value system instilled in your being then your decisions reflect what is going on . In order to use your time wisely you need to believe in yourself, believe in your purpose, and commit to using your time to accomplish those things in which you know belong to you. Because you believe in what it is you are here to do, you make plans, you avoid

Miguel Sanchez

distractions, you focus, and most of all you **value your time**. I value my time immensely! When you really , really learn that time is money you will begin to change your tune as to what you do with it.

All living things spend their lives doing 100% of what they were meant and supposed to be. For instance a tree spends all of its time driving its roots as deep as it possibly can and growing as tall as it possibly can. Have you ever heard of a tree growing only half as tall as it could? The difference between humans and all other species is that we have the ability to choose. Therefore whatever we do with our time is totally up to us and our greatest of all assets. From the moment we open our eyes in the morning we can choose as to what we are going to do. Some might say "oh I don't have a choice. I have to go to work". Well even that is a choice, you can choose never to go back to work at all if you want but of course it would come with consequences. It is the same with all of our choices in how we go about using our time- it all involves consequences. If you choose to stay home all day and play video games and watch mindless T.V. then that has its consequences also. This is all common knowledge, but I would like to add a small twist to what you do every day. Try keeping a time journal for at least one week. Now before you roll your eyes at this I completely understand that this is something that I know that you do not want to do-at all. However – once again it's up to you what you choose to do with your time. By taking on this task (in 15 minute intervals) you will allow yourself the ability to see exactly where your time goes and how much time you spend doing what. If improving your use of time is important to you and you want to make better use of it then you will choose to do it – if not you won't it's just that simple.

After completing this exercise ask yourself these questions.

1) Where am I spending most of my time?
2) What time am I getting up?
3) Is it possible to get up earlier to give yourself more time during the day?
4) What am I doing while I'm driving- could I be listening to self-improvement tapes or returning phone calls (voice calls – use a blue tooth)?

5) How much time do I spend just thinking or meditating?
6) How much time am I spending watching T.V.?
7) How much time am I spending with family?
8) How much time am I spending on social media?
9) How much time (consistently) do you allot yourself in working on your business plan, book, invention, or so on...?
10) What are you doing consistently with your time after you get off of work?
11) What do you spend your time doing on the weekends?
12) What do you do habitually?
13) How time do you spend planning-anything?

These questions are really just the beginning of being truthful with ourselves and maximizing our time here on this earth. The time we have is extremely finite and we all only have so much of it to accomplish what we were meant to do here during our presence here on the face of the earth. We must stop thinking of time as an amount of duration but think of it as an amount of Doo-ration!

Make It Happen

The hard part to all of this "time-management "is that it takes effort, commitment. Focus, control, discipline and fortitude. The only question you need ask yourself is how bad do you want it? That being said , that is simply the difference in getting things accomplished in your life by focusing on the time that you spend every day accomplishing small tasks and that you commit yourself to those daily habits and that eventually get you exactly where you and only you want to be.

I once read a story of a very wealthy man who was worth hundreds of millions of dollars. When asked for an appointment to have a conversation about an area of interest that he had, he gave the individual the time between 11:40 AM and 11:50 AM. He was so precise with his time that he scheduled these 10 minutes 2 weeks in advance because he knew exactly what he'd be doing each and every minute of his time every single day.

Let's make an example of a perfect day :
6:00 AM Rise and pray/ meditate

6:15 Exercise – while exercising listen to self-improvement tapes

7:15 Head home to get ready for work

8:45 AM arrive at work 15 minutes early

5:00 PM off work- Listen to self-improvement tapes on the way home

5-7:00 PM family time – dinner

7-8PM- reading self-improvement books, books on the field in which you have a gift in

8-9PM- Planning , your days , weeks , months , years

10-11PM- 20 minutes meditating , 20 minutes re-capping the day (what got accomplished what didn't , 10 minutes giving thanks for all that you have , 10 minutes visualizing yourself with all the things that want in life and how that life looks ...

Stay away from Distractions

There's almost an infinite amount of time wasters that exists in this world here are 10 to stay away from or manage appropriately:

Make It Happen

1) **T.V.**
2) **Procrastination**
3) **E-mail**
4) **Cell Phones**
5) **Interruptions**
6) **Small talk**
7) **People**
8) **People who want to waste your time with insignificant conversation**
9) **People who want you to do for them something that they could do themselves**
10) **Social Media** (A big one)

Once I started managing my time wisely, I started to notice that my bank account got bigger and bigger, especially when you work for yourself. When you're an entrepreneur you eat what you kill – so you can't spend a lot of time talking to the other Lions or you won't get to eat. I began doing the things that I'm telling you to do and my life started going in a whole different direction. This one skill set (and it is a skill) can change everything! I went from $86.00 to closing

Miguel Sanchez

multi-million dollar deals! I enjoy life to the fullest and it is my sincere hope that the information that you just read will help you achieve your wildest dreams!

About the Author

Born and raised in Washington D.C. , his father was a Cuban immigrant. His parents divorced when he was 1 and his father (who was a drug dealer) was murdered when Miguel was 10 years old. However the money left from his Fathers drug empire enabled Miguel to attend Military school where he became the 2nd highest ranking cadet in the school. After High School Miguel created an 11 year plan for his life that included becoming an Air Force pilot and becoming a Lawyer.

However It took Miguel 11 years to graduate with a 4 year Bachelor's Degree. After attending Tuskegee Institute (where he first encountered his fraternity Omega Psi Phi) he transferred to Howard University to be near his newly born son. Unable to continue to work 3 jobs and attend school full time as a single parent Miguel transferred to San Diego State University. From there he joined the U.S. Army where he joined the elite 82nd Airborne Division as a Paratrooper and finally finished his B.S. Degree in North Carolina at Campbell University . He went to school after duty hours in an attempt to complete his graduate education while also accomplishing 52 parachute jumps. While attending his Master's program he was sent to the Gulf War in operation Desert Storm for almost a year. During his tenure in the Army he took sole custody of his (then) 8 year old son and raised him as a single parent and then decided to leave the Army to pursue entrepreneurial goals.

Miguel Sanchez

He and his son moved to Atlanta after the war where he opened up what became the 3rd largest minority owned Mortgage Banking firm in the United States. As business goes the company took a downturn and his company was forced to shut down multiple offices.

Shortly thereafter he opened up a theme restaurant called "The Hip Hop Cafe" which many celebrities visited such as Ludicrous, Warren G, Mos Def, Swiss Beats, Goodie Mob, Outkast and many, many more. The restaurant made over 1 Million dollars in revenue the first year in business. That business allowed him to purchase and/or flip more than 30 properties. He worked 7 days a week at both businesses for several years until unfortunately the restaurant fell prey to rising labor and food cost and was forced to shut down.

From there he went back to school and completed his Master's Degree. He went to work in the post-secondary proprietary college education industry where he rose to the level of Director of Admissions for 16 Years. He was chosen as Corinthian Colleges' top 10 Directors in 2 Countries but decided to move to Las Vegas and to pursue his passion in Real Estate and public speaking where he now is a rising star at Wardley Real Estate. While at Wardley he has become #1 at his office and one of Wardley's top agents in the city of Las Vegas. By using the principles he has put together in his book he consistently found ways of rising to the top in whatever he chooses to do. In this book he encourages individuals to push through obstacles and find their true purpose in life and pursue that which you are given a gift to do.

Make It Happen

Follow Miguel here:

Twitter: https://twitter.com/miguels71404589/
Facebook: https://www.facebook.com/miguelsfortune
Trient Press: https://trientpress.com/miguel-sanchez

www.ingramcontent.com/pod-product-compliance
Lightning Source LLC
Chambersburg PA
CBHW010921230426
43673CB00025B/474/J